T0024719
Facing
the Lion

Facing the Lion

Memoirs of a Young Girl in Nazi Europe

Abridged Edition

Simone Arnold Liebster

Illustrations by the author

GM&A Publishing
Davenport, Iowa

Abridged Edition

GM&A Publishing
4004 Rodeo Road
Davenport, IA 52806
(563) 391-1819
facingthelion@facingthelion.com

NOTE TO EDUCATORS: A free study guide for *Facing the Lion* (Abridged Edition) is available online at www.facingthelion.com. The study guide includes whole-class activities, small-group exercises, and journal questions, as well as historical background, maps, and primary-source documents. Among the documents in the study guide are letters written by Simone and her parents, Nazi reports on the Arnold family, and chilling examples of Nazi propaganda. The study guide provides tools to facilitate a meaningful exploration of ethical dilemmas and identity issues.

Facing the Lion: Memoirs of a Young Girl in
Nazi Europe [abridged edition] / Simone Arnold Liebster

ISBN 978-1-937188-00-9

DEDICATION

I dedicate this book to my beloved father who surrounded us with so much loving attention and beauty, and who provided gentle authority, exemplary courage, and a sense of humor, making our home a haven of peace.

I dedicate it to my cherished Mum who led her "little one" and helped her to grow into a happy adult, comforting her and surrounding her with motherly love and patience.

And also to Adolphe Koehl, Dad's intimate friend, who so generously helped us to face our situation and whose exceptional courage and practical wisdom has enlightened my path.

And to my devoted Aunt Eugenie who sacrificed all her earnings and risked her life for us. She endeared herself to me like a second mother.

I shall not forget to dedicate this book to Marcel Sutter, whose life became an example for me and sustained me. He was a brother to me, a close friend.

I must include Charles Eicher, who encouraged me to go to New York. He put me in contact with my "Liebster" and got me started in a new full and fruitful life.

CONTENTS

HISTORICAL NOTE

During the period of National Socialism, the religious beliefs, teachings and actions of the Jehovah's Witnesses were a public proclamation that approximated a way of life whose central tenets collided with those of the National Socialist state. Here was a small group of some 20 to 25,000 "average Germans" and those from other regions incorporated into the Third Reich who were publicly proclaiming their belief in a kind of shadow state, which was in direct opposition to the Nazi regime. Here was a group, which rejected the racial laws of the state, the oath of allegiance to Adolf Hitler, the German salute, and the duty to take up arms for Germany.

We are familiar with the statistics: nearly 10,000 Jehovah's Witnesses imprisoned and at least 2,000 admitted to Nazi concentration camps of whom at least half were murdered, over 250 by beheading.

What we do not know as well is the day-to-day existence of this extraordinary group of committed men, women and children under the rule of National Socialist terror.

That is why Simone Arnold Liebster's autobiography is of such importance. It brings a name and a voice to these statistics. It tells the story of spiritual resistance to a monstrous evil, and does so through the eyes and memories of a child.

Those who resisted the forces of Nazi evil when a simple declaration of state loyalty would insure their well being, when a simple signature would free them from the hell of a labor or concentration camp and protect them from violence and murder, have earned a special place and a special admiration. They give us hope and a belief in the ultimate triumph of human good.

Simone Arnold Liebster must be counted among these special people.

— Abraham J. Peck,
Vice President of the Association of
Holocaust Organizations

FOREWORD

The autobiography of Simone Liebster, née Arnold, is a compelling story about her personal search for faith and identity that entailed difficult social, political, and religious choices in her childhood. Born in 1930 near Mulhouse in Alsace, then part of France, Simone Arnold Liebster grew up in an extended close-knit Catholic family during the 1930s—a decade of political and social unrest and uncertainty. Religious conformity was the norm in this overwhelmingly Catholic region. In 1938, Emma Arnold, Simone's mother, converted to the beliefs of Jehovah's Witnesses, despite family opposition. Subsequently, Simone's father, Adolphe Arnold, was also baptized as a Witness, and Simone converted while still a child, in 1941.

The areas of Alsace and Lorraine had been German between 1871 and 1918, reverting to French jurisdiction until mid-June 1940, when the region was again incorporated into the German Reich. Almost immediately, the Germans imposed their social and political values, rapidly excluding large numbers of so-called "undesirables," including Jehovah's Witnesses, who had no place in the German "new order." German again became the language of the region; soon nonconformists had to fear denunciations by neighbors as the bonds of civil society were undermined.

Simone's father, Adolphe, was arrested on September 4, 1941, less than one month after Simone had been baptized as a Witness. With his arrest, Simone and her mother faced mounting economic hardships since her father's wages had been confiscated at his arrest, his bank account impounded, and her mother denied a work permit. During the following two years, Simone and her mother secured food in exchange for small jobs.

After his arrest, Simone's father was initially imprisoned at the Schirmeck-Vorbruck internment camp in Labroque. This prison camp had been opened in mid-July 1940 "for individuals, whose behavior would damage German authority in the region" and "to teach disobedient elements in Alsace proper attitudes to work and the political order of the German Reich."* The list of so-called "undesirables" and "disobedient elements" followed the usual categories applied by the Germans in all occupied territories and also included Jehovah's Witnesses. Since their beliefs did not allow them to render unconditional obedience to any state, the Witnesses in Alsace and Lorraine were subjected to the same persecution that other Witnesses had been facing in Nazi Germany after 1933. Simone's father, Adolphe Arnold, was subsequently moved from Schirmeck to Dachau and Mauthausen-Gusen concentration camps, and later liberated in May 1945 at the Ebensee subcamp of Mauthausen.

After 1941, Simone came under increasing physical and psychological intimidation at school to conform to her classmates' behavior, since she had refused to use the "Heil Hitler" salute or to join the League of German Girls (*Bund deutscher Mädel*). Intimidation and retaliation extended to school-age Jehovah's Witness children both in Nazi Germany and in incorporated Alsace and Lorraine. When Witness children refused to enroll either in the Hitler Youth or the League of German Girls or to conform to the norms of Nazi social and political behavior, school officials removed them from parental custody and sent them to Nazi homes and juvenile correctional institutions.

More than 500 such minor Jehovah's Witness children in Nazi Germany were involuntarily separated from their parents after formal judicial proceedings. Simone's autobiography gives us explicit details about the lives of

*Gudrun Schwarz, *Die nationalsozialistischen Lager* (Frankfurt and New York: Campus, 1990), p. 88.

these children in a Nazi reform school during the war years. Parental custody and contact was suspended if a child was found guilty of immoral and dishonorable behavior—that is, not belonging to Nazi organizations. School officials, police, and juvenile and district courts ruled that Witness parents endangered their children's welfare by not conforming to the norms of a Nazified educational system and society. The subsequent fate of these children removed from their families has seldom been told in detail. Simone Arnold Liebster's memoirs enable us to understand more about the experiences of these children.

Simone Arnold was expelled from school after being subjected to physical and psychological brutality and pressures to conform. At the age of twelve, she was taken from her mother's custody and involuntarily transferred to the *Wessenberg Erziehungsanstalt,* a reform school, in Konstanz (Germany). Plunged into a world of persecution and lacking contact with her parents, Simone Arnold had to surrender her adolescence in order to survive. The world of childhood and adolescence is usually a time of growth and development. For children trapped under Nazi rule, life became an inverted world of shrinking horizons and terror.

Simone Arnold Liebster's autobiography restores individuality and identity to the otherwise anonymous victims of the Nazis and reveals her strength of will to maintain whatever normality was possible in her fight for physical and psychological survival. Her story is one of hope, strength, and courage. Despite the harsh and tragic Nazi period, Simone Liebster's narrative reveals her courage in maintaining her social and religious values. It is a story worth reading and enables us to understand the fate of Jehovah's Witness children during the Holocaust.

— Sybil Milton, former Senior Historian,
U.S. Holocaust Memorial Museum
Spring 2000

ACKNOWLEDGMENTS

I have told this story as accurately as I can remember it, but I am grateful to many people who helped me put my account in its present form. Among them are Germaine Villard, Françoise Milde, Adolphe Sperry and his granddaughter Virginie, and Esther Martinez, who all did historical research to confirm the events and places I remembered. I also compared notes with Rose Gassmann and Maria Koehl, who have vivid eyewitness recollections of their own. Mrs. Bautenbacher at the *Wessenberg'sche Erziehungsanstalt fur Mädels* and the staff at the city archives of Constance assisted in obtaining documents relating to my incarceration. Author Andreas Müller, who has written about my husband's story, also shared interesting background information with me about the activities of the Hitler Youth. Additional documentation and photographic material were supplied by the archives of the Watch Tower Society in Selters, Germany, Thun, Switzerland, and Brooklyn, New York. The *Cercle Européen des Témoins de Jéhovah Anciens Déportés et Internés,* of which I am a foundation member, also contributed archival material.

Claudia Walter, Daniel and Nadège Foucher, and Elaine Siegel did the important and tedious work of processing my manuscript. Werner and Michelle Ebstein and Norman Gaydon translated letters and documents for me. Suzanne Glesser applied her considerable creative talent in designing the artwork for the cover. Manuel Schortgen spent long hours processing my illustrations for publication in the Abridged edition. Rick and Carolynn Crandall and their colleagues patiently edited and drew together the various pieces into a coherent work.

The support of Fred Siegel, my publisher, whose positive attitude and backing have brought the project to reality has meant a great deal to me.

The urging of two wonderful friends, the late W. Lloyd Barry and John E. Barr, gave me the needed motivation to write my story.

I must acknowledge a very special debt to Jolene Chu who gave me an enormous amount of help—for illuminating discussions, for her careful review of the manuscript, for her efficient writing skills, and for her cheerfulness, which was a source of encouragement for me. This work has brought us together and has built strong ties between us. I have found in her a daughter who could chronicle my story as if it were her own heritage.

Finally, I owe special thanks to my dear husband Max for his exceptionally patient and loving support.

INTRODUCTION

There are events in life that you can't forget, things that make an indelible impression. I will never forget the time I looked into the eyes of Adolf Hitler. It was late spring of 1940. My friend Hélène and I were riding our bicycles between the towns of Oderen and Mulhouse, near the border between France and Germany. Suddenly, two motorcycles with sidecars came down the road. The men wore helmets that even covered their foreheads. A black car followed slowly behind. A chill ran down my back.

"Quick, Hélène! Hide!" I threw my bike into the ditch. "Quick! Get out of the way. We don't say 'Heil Hitler.' Hurry!"

We threw ourselves under a large bush. As the car drove by, we held our breath. Two officers sat in the back seat of the topless car. Next to the uniformed driver stood a man—it was Hitler. He was holding on to the front windshield with both hands. Slowly he turned his head in our direction. Terrified, I froze. Hitler was long gone before I had the strength to crawl out from under the bush. That evil look of his went down deep inside me. I knew that I had seen demon eyes.

We would not say "Heil Hitler" because "heil" means "salvation," and the salute was a way of publicly confessing that salvation proceeds from Hitler. But we were Jehovah's Witnesses, and our religious convictions would not let us accept Hitler or any other man as our Savior.

My family and I were fully aware of the danger posed by Hitler and his Nazi regime, which demanded total obedience, total submission. Like a vicious lion in greedy pursuit of its prey, the Gestapo hunted us down. Eventually, they came for me. I can vividly remember even the smallest details of the times when I faced the Nazi "Lion." That beast robbed me of my childhood.

Yet, my survival testifies to the fact that even young people can triumph over adversity, provided that their conscience is trained and that they learn high moral and ethical values. It is my heartfelt wish that my experience inspire others to face the "lions" in their lives with hope and courage. Here is my story.

CHAPTER 1

Life Between City and Mountain Farm

I could hardly wait for Dad to get home. He worked as an art consultant at a big fabric mill in town. This week he had the morning shift and would be home at two o'clock. I set out my paintbrushes and aquarelle colors, ready for my art lesson. I would have Dad all to myself. First, I would sit on his lap while he had a cup of coffee. Then, I planned to surprise him with his favorite Mozart adagio, which I had practiced over and over. After that would come the best part: Dad would help me work on the painting of three roses that I had started.

The bell rang. I hurried as fast as I could to open the door, leaped up to the big man's neck, and gave him a big kiss. His face pulled back abruptly, his chest stiffened, and his arms hung at his side. A voice from behind him gave out a shrill, "Heil Hitler!"

Instead of my dad, two Gestapo agents—the Nazi secret police—stood in the doorway. I dropped to my feet, horrified. What had they done with my dad? They pushed their way into our apartment and kicked at my little dog Zita. That terrifying day the Nazis started to tear apart my world, piece by piece. They took my father away to a concentration camp, and they threatened to come back for Mum and me. I never finished my painting of the roses. For a long time, I couldn't even bear to look at it. I hid the unfinished roses away at the bottom of the drawer. Just like my painting, my carefree childhood came to an abrupt end.

JUNE 1933

My earliest memories take me back to my first home—a cottage where I lived with my parents. I loved that place, surrounded by hedges and meadows. We lived in Alsace-Lorraine, a region right on the border of Germany and France. Throughout the centuries, armies had fought over the land.

I was almost three years old when we, and my little dog Zita, moved to the French city of Mulhouse. We lived on the third floor of the apartment building at 46 Rue de la mer rouge (Red Sea Street). Here in the city, I was not allowed to get close to the windows or go out to the street on my own. How sad for a little country girl—even the flowers on the balcony seemed like prisoners of their pots!

At least we often visited my grandparents' farm in a place called Bergenbach. In the midst of rocks and ferns stood my grandparents' house. Grandma was a very industrious woman who took care of all the animals and the fields while the men went off to work. Grandpa was a color mixer in the printing factory, and my Uncle Germain, who was deaf, hewed stone in a quarry. Grandma always worried that Uncle Germain might not get the message when the men were about to dynamite the rock. Whenever she heard a blast from the quarry, she would stop what she was doing and say a prayer for her son. Grandma was a devout Catholic.

Uncle Germain and I communicated easily. I enjoyed his lively homemade sign language. Uncle Germain was very close to Grandma, and because of her, he was very religious. So was I. I loved going with Grandpa to Mass. I secretly wished to become a saint so that I could be near God in heaven and could send help to people who were suffering on earth.

No. 46, Rue de la mer rouge

After church, Grandpa, Uncle Germain, and I would go to the café where all the men of the village gathered. I remember hearing a strange

Oil painting of Bergenbach by Adolphe Arnold

conversation one day about farm animals and Jews. "I bought a cow from the horse dealer." "Which one? The Jew or the Alsatian?" "From the Jew, and he cheated me again!" "Why don't you go to the Alsatian?" "Well, he's too expensive. He always exaggerates the quality and inflates the price of his animals. He is dishonest!" I couldn't follow their reasoning. Why did they hate Jews and yet prefer to buy from them? It didn't make any sense.

After church Grandma always cooked a wonderful Sunday dinner, including her special homemade pastries. We six shared a quiet meal together. But sometimes my Aunt Valentine, Uncle Alfred, and red-haired cousin Angele came to visit. Uncle Alfred would always start an argument and spoil our meal. He brought up the same subject over and over—the rivalry between the French and the Germans. That would start the war of words. Grandpa complained about the Germans, and Grandma criticized the French. She praised Germany's new leader Adolf Hitler.

Aunt Eugenie with Simone and Grandfather-Godfather Paul Arnold, August 1930

Father and Mother with Simone

From rear, left to right:: Mother, Father, Grandpa Remy, Aunt Eugenie, Grandma Marie, and Uncle Germain; Simone in center

Father, Mother, Uncle Alfred, Aunt Valentine, Simone, Angele

The summer drew to a close, and it was time to return to the city and get ready for my first day of school. Mum got busy at the sewing machine, and in no time she made me three beautiful blouses, one pink, one light blue, and one light green.

OCTOBER 1, 1936

The girls' school, a pink sandstone building, stood next to the church. I knew the way, but on my first day, Mother walked with me to school. My teacher, "Mademoiselle" (French for "Miss"), had light-gray hair, a round face, and deep-blue eyes. She assigned me to a place next to a girl named Frida, at a desk that was nearly new. I could tell right away the teacher liked me.

I made friends with Frida and with three other girls who lived on my street: Andrée, Blanche, and Madeleine. Frida had blond hair, rosy cheeks, and dark circles around her eyes. She was always shaking, as if she was cold or scared. Frida's blouses were baggy and frayed. She came from a poor family. On our walk home, her house came first. The shutters facing the street were always closed. I felt sorry for Frida. My mum always had a piece of bread with jam waiting for me after school, but no one ever had a snack ready for Frida when she got home.

At least the welfare children got milk and bread at school. Dad explained that the poor children had these advantages because in Mulhouse the socialist workers had fought for their rights. Suddenly I felt uncomfortable

May 1937, class picture

Simone, front, center
Andrée, 2nd row, 2nd from right; Blanche, 2nd row, 1st on right
Mademoiselle, 3rd row, 1st from right
Madeleine, Frida, 3rd row, 4th and 7th, from right, respectively

in my new pink blouse. I didn't want to be considered a "rich girl." I would give my jam-and-butter sandwich to Frida in exchange for her dry roll. In the school yard, the lime tree turned yellow and the wind snatched the leaves, playing with them before we could catch them for our toys. But Frida never chased them. Sometimes she couldn't stop coughing, and she stayed home from school whenever we had bad weather. Before long, the first snows of winter came, and we hardly saw her.

At Christmas time the Christ-child brought me just what I wanted—a doll! I named her Claudine. But when I returned to school, I found out that my friends Andrée, Blanche, Madeleine, and Frida had received only a little fruit and a few nuts for Christmas. Mum said it was because they were poor. I felt very angry at the Christ-child for giving the poor children almost nothing. It seemed so unfair!

In early spring the doctor told Frida that she had to stay home until her cough went away. I would pass by her house and call out her name, but the house stayed silent. When the weather turned warm, she still didn't come to school. One day I noticed some pots of nice white flowers in her backyard. At least someone had paid her a little attention, I thought, but I really missed her.

Simone with Claudine, her doll, Christmas 1936

"Why can't Frida come to school?" I asked Mademoiselle. "Is she still coughing?" Instead of answering me, she caressed my hair.

"No, she's not coughing anymore. She's in heaven now."

Then I realized why I had seen the pots of flowers. A few days later, I walked past Frida's home. The shutters were closed; the flowers were withered—they too had died. I started to cry. I felt so sad, but I was also relieved for her. She wouldn't cough anymore but would sit on a cloud and play a harp.

Mum explained to me that Frida had died of a sickness called tuberculosis. I decided that I should become a nurse so that I could inform my classmates about the dangers of tuberculosis and other diseases. When my parents weren't watching, I would take Dad's doctor book down from the bookshelf and read it secretly.

Not long after Frida died, Mum bought a Bible and started to read it every day. She began to question some of the things we had learned in church. Dad was very unhappy, saying that the job of teaching religion belonged to the priests. My parents had a big argument one night, and Dad said Mum wasn't allowed to teach me about her ideas. I was furious. He treated me like a baby—I was seven years old!

After all, my parents had always taught me that I should think for myself. For instance, one day Mum took me to the fabric store to let me pick out material for my new Sunday coat. The saleslady showed us some fabrics and said, "These are in style; everybody chooses this one or that one."

But Mum bent toward me and said, "You choose, Simone. But remember, you don't want to be like everybody else; you want to be you. Ladies do not copy, they create."

The saleslady stared at us, astonishment showing in her eyes. "You are very young to make a personal choice," she said finally.

"Please show us those," I said, pointing to some bolts of fabric. Mum put aside some that were too expensive and let me choose from among the others. I picked out my own coat material. It was so exciting!

I couldn't understand why Dad wouldn't want Mum to teach me. He was the one who always talked about "conscience," a voice inside me that would tell me right from wrong. My inner voice told me that even though Dad had forbidden it, I should learn from the Bible. I begged Mum to teach me. Finally, Mum said, "Dad wouldn't forbid us to read from a Catholic Bible, would he?" She bought a new Bible that had approval signatures from Catholic bishops and cardinals on the first page. She read a few verses to me every day and told me that I should compare it with what I heard at church. Some nights after I had gone to bed, I would hear my parents in the parlor arguing about religion. For a while Dad stopped talking to us altogether. But as time passed, Dad began to take an interest in what Mum was learning.

He started to study the Bible himself, and he decided that Mum was right after all.

In school during our religious education class, the priest talked about the Nativity, the day God came down to earth and chose Bethlehem in the land of the Jews as his birthplace. But they had no room, no house for him or for Mary and Joseph. The holy family had to go to a stable, and Jesus had to be warmed up by the breath of a cow and a donkey. "And remember," the priest said, "the Jews killed Jesus, the incarnated God, and they asked that his blood come upon their children. That is why the Jews are condemned for eternity."

Because of their studies in the Bible, my parents decided that they would not be Catholics anymore. We stopped going to church. Instead of attending the priest's catechism class at school, I went to the principal's office and had civics lessons. One day after catechism class, a group of children surrounded me, shouting, "Heathen, you're a heathen!" "You don't go to church anymore. You're a Communist!"

"I am not," I shouted. "I'm a Christian!" I tried to explain what I had learned from reading the Bible with Mother. But a woman across the street called out, "Escape—she is dangerous!" All the children ran away screaming, even Blanche, Madeleine, and Andrée.

When I got to the street corner, another group of children confronted me. Some of the boys circled around me, calling me "dirty Jew, dirty Jew!" Why do they call me a Jew, and why dirty? I wasn't either one! Passersby finally chased the children away.

At home, Mother read me some Bible verses from the Gospels about persecution and insults. But I wanted to know, "Why did they call me 'dirty Jew'?" Our butcher was Jewish, and he was very clean. Mother liked him because he was honest and kind.

Sitting on my father's lap, I learned the meaning of the insult. My parents explained: "As you learn more about history, you'll find out that so-called Christians wouldn't let Jews have jobs as craftsmen. They had to live in special sections of town, and people accused them of killing God."

"I heard that. The priest told us about it."

"But God, whose name is Jehovah, never came to earth; nor was he killed by men. He doesn't make a distinction between races, colors, rich or poor; God is fair. God is love. Those who do not follow this teaching are under the power of evil and can say and do bad things, thinking they are right."

Little by little, the children tired of chasing me on the street. I had told them that Jesus, the Son of God, was a Jew and that being called a Jew is something honorable. All the apostles and Bible writers were Jews, and I wanted to be like them.

My schoolmates were not the only ones who didn't like our new religious beliefs. Mademoiselle started ignoring me. Grandma threatened to disown Mum for leaving the church. Aunt Eugenie, Mum's sister, said we had been misled. One day our neighbor Mr. Eguemann, a heavy drinker, threatened Dad, saying he should be killed for being a traitor to the church. He even chased Dad down the street with an ax, but Dad managed to get away. We steered clear of Mr. Eguemann after that.

We started attending meetings held by Jehovah's Witnesses, also called Bible Students.* A few families met at the city hall and discussed the Bible together. I enrolled in a class for children and received my very own Bible with a black cover and red edges. How I treasured it!

---

*In German, *Bibelforscher.*

Mum often visited our neighbors to read the Bible to them and to give them booklets. I often went along. Sometimes I even went by myself to talk to the farmers. We talked about the hope that some day God will make the earth into a paradise and even those who die, like my friend Frida, will live again. The conversations we had with people were so interesting. We would discuss them at home around our table.

I came to love our little congregation of Witnesses. I had two young playmates, André Schoenauer and Edmund Schaguené. I also gained a surrogate grandpa—Mr. Huber, a gentle, white-haired man with a golden chain attached to a watch in his vest pocket. Marcel Graf was an office clerk at the potassium mines—he was tall and bald, and he loved to talk.

Among our many friends, one couple was really special—the Koehls. They had a barber shop in the nicest part of town. One day when they were invited to our house, I eagerly waited for them at the window. They came in spite of the freezing weather, both looking like they had stepped out of a fashion magazine. Adolphe, who had the same name as my father, gently held his wife Maria's elbow with one hand and led their dog by the leash with the other. Maria's hands were tucked in a fur muff that matched her silver fox collar. Seated in our little parlor, the two Adolphes got into a spirited conversation. Meanwhile, Mum and Maria exchanged recipes in the kitchen. I tried to listen to both conversations, but my ears tuned in on Dad and Adolphe.

"Who does he think he is—a god?" one said to the other.

"He's just a puppet in the hands of the demons," the other answered.

"He claims to be Germany's savior. He's just a worm."

"A very harmful, rotten worm."

"He gains victory after victory."

"He does, but he will never prevail over Jehovah's Witnesses."

I wondered who they were talking about. In the center of the conversation was a book that the Koehls had brought, *Crusade Against Christianity.** It lay open to a drawing of some kind of camp.

"The information we learn from this book is very important. It will help us to become cautious like a serpent and yet innocent like a dove," said one of the Adolphes. The other agreed.

As the Koehls departed, they left a big emptiness. I somehow felt that I now had another set of parents.

---

*The 1938 book *Kreuzzug gegen das Christentum* (Crusade Against Christianity) described the Nazi persecution of Jehovah's Witnesses, who had been banned in Germany since 1933. The book had diagrams of the Nazi camps Esterwegen and Sachsenhausen.

CHAPTER 2

The Threat of War

"Grandpa, are we going to have a war?"

"Hard to say, but I hope not."

"Our class went on an outing to the mountain that we can see from our balcony. We saw a rusty helmet right by where we were sitting. And when I went to have a closer look, I found a skull inside it!"

Grandpa looked at me somberly with his blue eyes. "It was the site of the greatest battle between the French and the Germans during the Great War. Thousands died there."

"Grandpa, tell me—was he young? Did he have children? How did he die? By a bullet or a bayonet? Was he French or German? Catholic or Protestant?"

"It doesn't really matter, Little One. He was just a man. Hatred, Simone, is stronger than reason. Hatred, bitterness, and vengeance can poison people."

Listening to the news on the radio became a very serious matter. Everyone sat there in almost religious silence. Then Grandma started accusing the French of trying to provoke a war. Grandpa blamed everything on the Germans. The arguments at the table started up again about Danzig, Poland, Albania, and the Anschluss (the takeover of Austria by Germany on March 13, 1938). Grandpa looked at me and said: "That's far from here, Simone. Don't worry." But Aunt Eugenie explained to me that because Alsace was such a desirable land, Germany and France had fought over it like two dogs would fight over a bone. War might come here again for the third time in 70 years!

FALL 1939

On September 1, Hitler's armies invaded Poland. War in Alsace seemed a greater threat than ever. The closing days of summer brought changes to the people of Alsace. Many families moved away from the area near the German border. Even Angele, my cousin and best playmate, left for Vichy, where her father's factory was relocated. For me, the autumn brought a change in schools. With the encouragement of Mr. Huber, the presiding minister of our Bible Student congregation, as well as the Koehls, I started taking advanced classes. I had to leave all my friends at the *Volksschule*. In the new school of higher learning, the *Mittelschule,* my playmates and new friends were Daniele and her cousin Anita. Mum studied the Bible with their mothers.

I went shopping with Mum. In the marketplace, people were loaded down with heavy bags. The smoked meat sold out early that morning. The supplies of flour, rice, and cereals were all gone too. Clusters of grave-looking people stood around murmuring. The sunny, late-summer day seemed gloomy somehow.

At the weekly meeting of our congregation, we found the gloom mirrored on the faces. We learned that the French government had put the work of Jehovah's Witnesses under ban.* Freedom of speech, freedom of press, freedom of assembly would all be taken away.

How sad to learn that we would be able to gather only in small groups. Many of us wouldn't see one another anymore! Tears ran down our cheeks when Adolphe Koehl said: "Liberty may be banned—but not our faith. Equality is denied by man, not by God. Fraternity will keep us together in spite of the ban." We hugged one another sadly.

*In mid-October 1939, the French government banned Jehovah's Witnesses, who numbered about 1,000 in France.

Alfred Zinglé decided to move out of Alsace. "I'd rather move to the interior on the other side of the border in the Vosges Mountains. Maybe I can set up a connection to smuggle some Bible literature across the border."

Marcel Graf, Adolphe Koehl, and Dad would begin organizing the secret "underground" activity. "It would be a big advantage to be underground already should the Germans take control of Alsace," said Adolphe. All 45 members of our congregation dispersed, and we withdrew from our public activity.

❧ ❧ ❧

War didn't dominate my parents' thoughts. Our daily life didn't change much. Dad still made us laugh, and he read to me about faraway places. He played games with me and Zita like always. At the same time, Dad wanted to be sure that I was prepared for what might happen.

"If Hitler takes over the country, we will be confronted with a serious problem. He demands total obedience and acts of idol worship, such as the greeting 'Heil Hitler.' 'Heil' means 'salvation,' so the 'Heil Hitler' salute is a way of acknowledging that salvation proceeds from him.

"Remember the story of King Nebuchadnezzar and the three Hebrews who refused to worship the king's golden image, and you'll see why the first Christians refused to burn incense in the name of the emperor. You'll be able to decide what to do if you are confronted with a similar situation. We are servants of Jesus Christ, and we bear the name of his Father, Jehovah. Our Savior will never be Hitler or any other man."

Dad helped me to understand that God doesn't want us to worship images of any kind. He encouraged me to follow my conscience, even if people pressured me to do something wrong. I should listen to my inner voice, he said, just like the three brave Hebrew boys in Babylon listened to theirs. I loved that story. Mother would describe vividly how they had refused to bow down to the king's statue and how God had saved them when they were thrown into the fiery furnace. I got the point of Dad's lesson: Never give to anyone or to anything else the things that belong to God.

Mum and Dad had both been baptized, symbolizing their promise to be witnesses for God. I wanted to be baptized too, but my parents thought I was too young. They also knew that it would soon become more difficult, even dangerous, to be Jehovah's Witnesses.

In May of 1940, the German troops crossed the Belgian border and marched into northern France. In mid-June the news on Swiss radio said that Paris had fallen into the hands of the Germans. That morning, Grandma decided to go to a lookout point and listen to the news from the town crier. She took me along. From the edge of the cliff, we could see the whole valley.

"Look, Grandma, on the church belfry, there's a red flag with a white circle and something in it."

"It's the German flag with the swastika," Grandma said excitedly. From this spot I could see the same kind of flag on the belfries of the churches of the nearby towns Krüth, Felleringen, and Wesserlingen. But hanging outside the main window of the city hall, the French flag still flew—a true picture of Alsace, the divided land.

CHAPTER 3

Return to the Reich

The shadow of Germany's iron hand could be felt everywhere as Hitler restored Alsace to the German empire, the "Third Reich." All over the country, the German soldiers strutted, their belt buckles proclaiming *Gott mit uns,* or "God is with us." The gray lines of uniformed soldiers marched, their boots pounding down the streets. Their boastful songs filled the air as they looted the shops. At night, truckloads of merchandise from Jewish stores left for Germany. Some people said that it was fair that Jewish riches be returned to the nation from which they were "stolen." My parents said: "It's bare-faced larceny. Adolf Hitler is a representative of the Devil."

One warm day in June 1940, Hitler came to see for himself the land that now lay at his feet. On that frightening day, my friend Hélène and I nearly came face-to-face with his procession. We were riding our bicycles near the border between France and Germany. Seemingly out of nowhere, soldiers on motorcycles appeared on the road, heading slowing in our direction. Behind them came a black car. A chill ran down my back.

"Quick, Hélène! Hide!" We threw our bikes into the ditch. "Quick! Get out of the way. We don't say 'Heil Hitler.' Hurry!"

We dived under a large bush full of thorns. As the car passed by, we held our breath. My heart pounded so wildly that I thought my eardrums would burst. As we lay flat on our stomachs in the grass, I dared to look up.

A man stood erect next to the uniformed driver. Hitler! He had a proud face made of stone, with a straight nose underlined with a black mustache, tight lips,

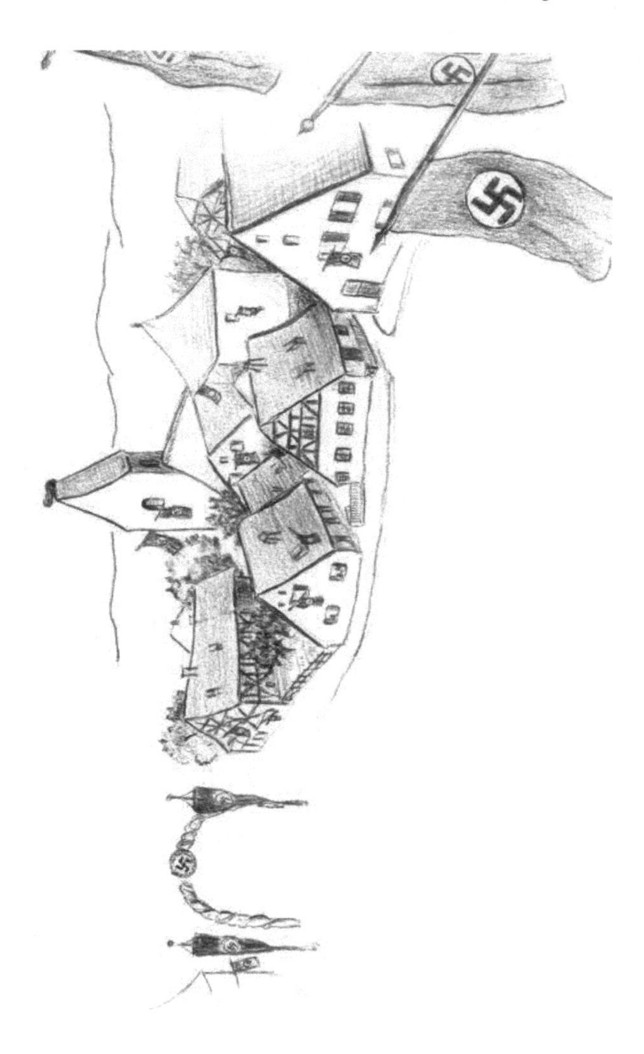

clenched teeth. He slowly turned his head in our direction. His eyes were piercing, icy, like demon eyes.

Hitler and his soldiers were long gone before we dared to crawl out from under the bush. I knew I would never forget that evil look. In the classrooms, in the businesses, his picture hung everywhere, but I saw only his eyes.

Swelling victory reports on the radio caused the morale of some Alsatian people to sink. At the same time, underground political movements sprang up. Arrests mounted; so did hatred and nationalism. The attempt to turn independent Alsatians into true Germans was a lost cause from the beginning.

❧ ❧ ❧

The Nazis set up Schirmeck-Vorbruck camp in 1940 to reeducate stubborn Alsatians. A six-week sentence in the camp usually stripped a person of 30 to 50 pounds, after which he was either released or was transferred to another Nazi camp, such as Dachau or nearby Struthof. The camp at Struthof sat on top of the mountain. Its crematory chimney stood tall against the sky and served as a warning to those in the Schirmeck camp.

When we saw an emaciated man in the street, hugging the walls, we knew that he had come out of Schirmeck. We also knew that he was forbidden to tell about life inside the camp. We Jehovah's Witnesses had to be cautious—we were members of a religion under ban. We knew we could end up in Schirmeck too.

We needed a hiding place for our underground activity. During the first ban in France, Alfred Zinglé smuggled Bible literature by bicycle from the French valley of the Vosges Mountains, hiding it in the frame of his bicycle. But now with the Germans on patrol, it was much more dangerous. Another way had to be found.

Dad wiped the sweat from his forehead and looked at a map. The sun beat down on us as the winding road climbed up the steep hillside. We walked toward a park made up of individual garden plots, each with its own little shed. We left our bikes at the entrance. I tied Zita on her leash and headed to a corner plot. Adolphe and Maria Koehl were expecting us.

Adolphe Koehl, c. 1950

"What do you think?" my father asked the other Adolphe.

"Yes, it seems possible to hold our secret meetings here. The place is really quite isolated." Maria could see a long way down the street, and if anybody were to stand behind the house to spy on us, the dog would bark. The next garden was abandoned.

❧ ❧ ❧

Soon school would start—German school! Knowing how the Nazi regime treated people, even children, I started to grow more and more tense. But I was determined never to heil, to accept Hitler as Savior. I knew I had to be careful.

The first day at school was reassuring. I had the same seat as the previous year. The class was twice as big. I felt relieved. The door to the classroom was situated in such a way that I could hide when the teacher entered the class. He would say "Heil Hitler," and the class had to stand with arms outstretched and shout "Heil Hitler" in reply.

"My name is Zipf," said the tall, gray-haired teacher in perfect German. He stated in a clipped voice: "Class will be from 8:00 a.m. to 1:00 p.m., as is done in Germany. Only German will be spoken. The first months will focus on the German language and arithmetic; every other course is put off until later. It is our aim to make you into German citizens. You must show respect for any superior in class by giving the German greeting 'Heil Hitler' with an outstretched arm. If you meet a superior on the street, you must lift the forearm with the palm erect."

A new problem! Hiding behind tall girls was possible in class, but on the street? Every walk was nerve-racking.

A *Gauleiter* was a Nazi Party district leader. Mr. Zipf admonished us: "*Gauleiter* Wagner wants you to become true Germans, productive members of the Third Reich, which will live for at least 1,000 years. Together, we will build the Holy Roman Empire of the German nation!"

The next day we had our first lesson on reading and writing *Sütterlin*—an old-style German script brought back during the Nazi occupation. We were told to copy the words from the German national hymn and another song that had been written on the blackboard. As I wrote the anthem's words *Deutschland über alles in der Welt*, meaning "Germany above everything in the world," I knew I could never sing it. For me, the Kingdom of God was above everything in the world. The other song, *Horst-Wessel Lied,* memorialized a Nazi storm trooper who was killed by political enemies and was now revered as a Nazi martyr. It was the marching song of the Nazi Party. But never would I march with them.

Evolution was the next subject to be introduced. With diagrams and charts, we learned the theory of natural selection. They said the strong, who are better stock, eliminate the weak. But I didn't agree. My grandparents didn't kill the weaker animals but treated them kindly. They would even make herb tea for them, and the animals grew to be strong and healthy.

Soon we had another big poster hanging on the classroom wall. It was a picture of four heads. To the left were a couple of "True German Aryans"; to the right, two faces of some "primitive" African tribespeople. In between was the question: "How could the same soul and the same spirit abide in these different bodies?" We were taught that the Aryan race had fought to become superior, leaving the others far behind. We had a sacred inheritance because our forefathers had given their blood for their fatherland. We were to preserve it by keeping free from the *Untermenschen* (subhumans). They could weaken our superiority, the purity of our race. Another chart showed a list of races represented by photographs, starting with the German race on the top and the *Untermenschen,* comprising Jews, Poles, Russians, and Africans, at the bottom.

❧ ❧ ❧

People lived under constant pressure. The German authorities had woven a tight spy network, requiring people to turn in the names of those who didn't go along. Right from the beginning, Adolphe the barber found himself in a dreadful situation. A German policeman came for a haircut. As he sat down, he said: "I was notified that you haven't followed the order to hang up Hitler's picture. It's required by law. If you don't, we'll close down your business." Adolphe gave the officer a perfect haircut, and the policeman let the subject drop.

A high-ranking SS officer came into the barbershop. As he entered, he shouted, "Heil Hitler!" All the men in the barbershop trembled.

"Guten Tag," said Adolphe.

"I said Heil Hitler!"

"Oh yes, I heard you."

"Heil Hitler is the German greeting!"

"Guten Tag is also a German greeting, and since

Germany is a freedom-loving nation, I choose to use this greeting." The barber's hand was precise, his conversation self-controlled. He cut the man's hair, massaged his scalp with lotion, brushed his jacket, and handed him his hat.

"Heil Hitler!"

"*Auf wiedersehen.*"

"I said Heil Hitler! This is the German greeting!"

"Well, *Auf wiedersehen* is certainly not a French greeting. For me it is a matter of conscience—Germany certainly respects freedom of conscience."

The SS officer walked out, spun back around, and said, "You'll hear from us!"

The SS came back; and other officials came—all for haircuts. A quiet terror hung in the air. There wasn't a day without some incident.

The winter passed by slowly. It had been very cold and snowy, bringing hardship on many people. It had also interrupted our secret connections with Alfred Zinglé. No border crossings were possible. In those months, school was a quiet haven of learning for me. I hid behind the tall girls, and no one noticed that I didn't give the Hitler salute. My strategy worked perfectly.

Movies, the theater, musical performances—these were only for Nazis, their friends, and compliant people. The swastika flag, the national anthem, and the "Heil Hitler" choruses colored every program.

Arrest hung over our heads as a daily threat. As the pressure grew, so did our caution. In the evening, we would leave the light and the radio on whether we were home or not. We walked Zita in the daytime, and we left our bikes in the garage. We learned to tiptoe quietly and without a word. When leaving the apartment, we looked around—under porches, behind doors, in trees—in case a hidden informer was watching us. To my delight, Aunt Eugenie had also become a Bible Student, and she joined us in our secret activities.

❧ ❧ ❧

APRIL 11, 1941

The day came for our most important celebration—the annual Memorial of Christ's death. It was our first one under German occupation. We had a code name for the Nazi police. We called them the "Lion." We realized that in Germany the Gestapo would lie in wait on that special day. They knew that all of Jehovah's Witnesses would courageously gather after sunset. Now it was our turn. How many of us would the Lion catch this time?

Dad had me do the research to determine the correct date for the Memorial, the 14th of Nisan (Passover) according to the Jewish calendar. Mum made her weekly trip to the grocery store and then brought the groceries to our secret meeting place, at Mrs. Straub's home. Mother took care of Mrs. Straub, and I often went along. The elderly grandma always sat at her window to keep watch for us. She had lots of wrinkles and sparkling gray eyes. When she talked, no teeth showed.

Mrs. Straub had a humble home. It was our first time meeting at her place. Watching from behind her curtains, she could see everything going on down the street, yet she couldn't be seen from outside. At set times, one by one, people arrived quietly. Dad was the last to come. He kept watch outside and finally came in when no one was around. A serene feeling filled my heart.

We all knew that there could be a police raid at any moment. But it meant so much to us to commemorate the death of Jesus. On the table sat the red wine and the unleavened bread, reminding us that Jesus had sacrificed his life for humankind. Many shed tears of emotion during the quiet talk. We could only read the words of our song together softly, but prayer united our hearts. Then everyone left silently, just the way they had come. We were the last to leave.

My parents talked about how grateful they were to be together still. I looked at them in the bright light of the full moon. We stopped in a grove where beautiful blossoms covered the apple trees. There I declared to my astonished parents: "I want to be baptized. I want to belong exclusively to Jehovah and his Son. You have no right to say no!"

❧ ❧ ❧

Dad listened with delight to my piano playing. Then he hugged Mum, kissed me, and waved good-bye. He would be back before dark. A light summer rain was falling. I watched him disappear around the corner, going in the opposite direction of where he needed to go. He was going to hold a secret Bible meeting in a ladies' tailor shop. It should have taken only two hours. Two hours came and went. I climbed into bed but lay there wide-awake. I felt Mum's restlessness. Dad hadn't come home; surely she knew why. I got out of bed.

"Has Papa been arrested?"

She said a prayer to calm me down, and then she brought me back to bed, tucked me in, and opened the shutters to let some cool air into the warm room. A creak of the wooden stairs filled me with terror. The footsteps stopped in front of the apartment door. A noise? A key? The door opened slowly. I strained in the dark to see who had entered. The light came on. It was my father. What a relief!

A young man named Marcel Sutter had been the cause of Dad's delay, and the following evening we would get to meet him. He claimed to be an atheist. He had been in the French army, in the air defense. He was an electrical-engineering student. After the meeting, Marcel had waited for Dad. At first Dad was hesitant, but the young man said that he just had a few questions. They searched for a place to talk in secret. At the end of that first conversation, Marcel said, "This is the truth!" Dad's enthusiasm made me like the 22-year-old lad before I ever met him!

Marcel, a handsome young man, stood in our hallway. From my room I could scrutinize him in the hallway mirror. He really was just the way Dad had described him. He was calm and poised as they talked; he listened respectfully to Dad.

Marcel's visits became a habit. He and Dad shared the same thirst for spiritual answers, yet they also discussed geography and astronomy. Marcel had found in my dad a real father. But before leaving our house, he never failed to ask me to sit at the piano and play a piece by Mozart or Schubert.

CHAPTER 4

Sudden Dangers

JUNE 1941

The weather was burning hot. We tried to keep the temperature under control by closing the shutters and hanging wet sheets over the open window. The next day was the first Sunday of the month, the appointed day to pick up the literature that Alfred Zinglé would leave at a secret hiding place.

My parents, worried about the weather and the danger, got up several times during the night and at last decided we would attempt the rendezvous. Adolphe the barber came along. We rode the train up to the mountain range where three valleys came together. The third valley was on the French side. Alfred Zinglé had moved there. On the Alsatian side of the border, a three-mile safety zone had been established, and a special pass was required for anyone traveling there. The checkpoints were very strict, but it was Alfred who had the most delicate task—the actual border crossing along the mountain summit. The soldiers in field-gray uniforms patrolled the borders constantly.

We all looked like mountain climbers, with walking sticks, backpacks, and hiking shoes. In several places the brooks had overrun their banks and flooded our path. We took the shorter and steeper path through the forest, but the detour delayed us. The slippery, wet fir needles slowed us down.

We came out above a little lake called Sternsee—Lake of the Stars. The glassy water lay in a crater surrounded by forest and cascades of fallen rocks. Our path curved around the lake and reached the rocky side, which was barren and full of caves. We found the cave where Alfred had hidden the literature.

Quickly, I ran inside to undress. I wore a girdle Mum had sewn for me. I had begged my parents to let me carry the forbidden Bible literature—*The Watchtower*. Finally Mum had agreed and had sewn a double back in my girdle, forming a secret pocket. While Mum spread out the picnic, the literature was quickly tucked away. A noise caught our attention, a shadow of a man frightened us. Suddenly Alfred stood before us. He had come back to see if we had made it.

Mum looked at the clouds piling up on top of the mountain. She said, "We'd better leave as soon as possible—before the weather catches us and makes it hard for us to make our way down." We said a prayer together inside the cave, and then we parted. Alfred climbed back up toward the border, and we ran down, glancing once in a while at the mountaintop behind us. Chilly air fell over us, but Mum decided to stop for a while. We waited to see if we heard any voices or saw a sentinel.

"It seems that Alfred made it across the border, but you see those clouds jumping over the mountain top? They are galloping in our direction just like a cavalry. Hurry before the fog overtakes us!" A breathless run brought us to the Riesenwald. The fir-tree forest had become inhospitable and gloomy. But we kept on going, running over rocks and water, splashing mud in every direction. As soon as we could see the green meadows, we slowed down. Soon we would find the path.

We had almost come to the crossroad when a sharp call stopped us in our tracks. "Halt!" In front of us stood two soldiers. We all stood stiff except for Mum, who right away waved and shouted: "We need help. We're lost!" She slowly advanced toward the pointed guns, showing them her pass, the one for the other valley.

"The fog is terrible! We want to go to Urbès Storckenson." That was the village for which we had the necessary papers. After checking our papers, the soldiers said they needed a closer investigation. We were to follow them. We had to climb up again. No one spoke. I was cold and sore, and my belly ached.

The path ended at a farm. We entered the house. The room looked like a chimney, full of soot. The lady inside took one look at me and said, "My poor child, you look green." I was sick, holding my belly with both hands. She gave me a cup of hot sugar water with some alcohol in it. She brought me into the stable. "Lie down on the hay. You'll warm up very fast!" No sooner had I warmed up than I fell asleep. The Germans searched the others thoroughly, even down to their shoes and socks, while I slept soundly.

When Mum woke me, I heard the soldiers' order: "Go right down to the valley. Don't stop anywhere; take the next bus." We ran down as fast as we could. When we reached the vicinity of Rimbach, we thanked Jehovah for his guidance.

Dad decided to do a painting of Mum's beautiful blossoming cactus to capture its exceptional splendor. As for me, I felt inspired by the three roses mother had placed in a vase on the lace cloth. Dad gave me my first expensive aquarelle paper. Gradually, under his guidance, three roses, two yellow and one red, began to take shape. But before I ever finished my first painting, Aunt Eugenie invited me to go with her to Bergenbach to give my grandparents a helping hand.

Bergenbach, with the cool brook, the jumping grasshoppers, and the colorful butterflies, was a world without fear. Wandering through its rugged rocks and dark pine forests and listening to the music of the wind, I soon forgot all the pressures of the city. Climbing up and perching on some rocks, discovering new mountains on the horizon, looking down on the villages tied to each other by a twisting road, I was far away in another world. I was in paradise. Beautiful Bergenbach!

In my heart, in my mind, I saw paintings everywhere. But Dad advised me first to finish what I had started. The roses—I had put off finishing the roses. For now, I had to store away deep in my heart the paradise scenery of Bergenbach.

CHAPTER 5

The Lion Strikes

SEPTEMBER 1941

I was back in school. It was a relief for all of us to have the routine that school provided. I had the same teacher. I had come to appreciate Mr. Zipf because he was strict but mild-tempered. I was also in the same classroom, in the same seat.

We learned how to identify races and their places of origin as well as their behavior. We saw how to measure their foreheads, skulls, noses, and chins. Another teacher, a lady, instructed us in the subject of maternity and child rearing. A textbook taught us the need to keep blood pure. Girls had the privilege of childbearing—to be mothers of the coming nation. The best men would be selected to father their children. These children would become an elite class.

Dad had the morning shift that first week of school. So he spent time with me in the afternoon, checking my new schoolbooks. He told me, "Humankind is like a garden, full of different colors and shapes, all to its Creator's glory." We looked at the section in my textbook that discussed evolution. Dad liked to ask me questions. He said: "If selective breeding were the way to help mankind, wouldn't Jesus have used this method? After all, Jesus healed the sick and disabled."

SEPTEMBER 4, 1941

One afternoon in the middle of the week, I got out my unfinished painting of the roses and waited eagerly for Dad to come home. The bell rang—Mum had forgotten to unlock the door. I ran to open the door and jumped up to hug him.

The Unfinished Roses

"Gestapo!" The stabbing sound of those syllables fell like an ax. Mother came. Without being invited, two men pushed their way in. The one I had kissed ended up in Dad's armchair; the smaller one gave a light kick in the direction of Zita's snarling teeth before sitting opposite his crony. They sent me to my room and ordered Mum to take a seat where the sunlight would shine in her face.

They asked what her religion was. Mum answered with a calm, firm voice, "Jehovah's Witness."

On the shelf in my room was the *Elberfelder* Bible, a German edition of the Holy Scriptures. It had God's name, Jehovah, in it, and the Nazis regarded Jehovah as the name of the Jewish god. We would be arrested if those men found it. I went to Mum and said, "Mum, I can't do my homework. I need a notebook."

Dark Gestapo eyes stared at me. "Go and get one."

"Come back right away," ordered the second one.

"Get one at Aline's shop. Tell her I'll pay later, and take my black bag," added Mum. I put the *Elberfelder* Bible in her bag. My heart started beating faster and faster. I went out the back door. No one was around. I went into our neighbor's garden among the rows of dense vegetables. I hid the Bible under a bean bush.

Aline was surprised to see me at that hour of the day. She silently handed me a notebook. As I walked home, my legs felt like lead. People looked out from behind their curtains at the Gestapo car. They drew back when they saw me.

In our shed, I spotted Dad's bike. Dad is home! He will save us! I sprouted wings. I bolted upstairs with relief, only to find Mum sitting as I had left her. I collapsed against the wall. I knew then that Dad had been arrested.

From where I stood, I could see the living room reflected in the hallway mirror. I heard some of the interrogation. Mother's calmness brought my confidence back. I saw the men write Mother's answers down in a huge book; they put a mark by some answers. When they asked, "Do you have *Watchtower* magazines?" to my surprise, Mum answered yes.

"Where did you get them from?"

"I got them before the war."

"Where do you have meetings?"

"Before the French government banned us, we met on Canal Street."

"I'm talking about now!"

"No, we can't rent a hall."

"But you gather secretly!"

"What's secret? Anyone can follow me wherever I go."

Teatime had passed, and Mother was not allowed to move. They questioned her for more than three hours.

I really got afraid when I heard them say: "We put you under oath! Turn in the names of other Bible Students!" Mother sat silent for a long time.

"We have no time!" one screamed. I shivered.

In a soft voice Mother said slowly: "Sorg, Knoerry, Harbeck, Kulame, Gertz. Some others I have forgotten." Shaking all over, I felt sick, stunned by Mum's confession. The one man angrily slammed the huge notebook shut.

"You are a cunning creature!" he hollered. Then I realized that Mum had named well-known Witnesses who had died or who lived in other countries.

"If you want to see your husband, remember that he is in our hands," the taller man said. The shorter one added: "You and your daughter will have the same fate. We're going to come back and arrest you." Their heavy boots stamped downstairs. Mother stood at the landing. A cold voice came up the stairs, "You'll never see your husband again, never!"

Mother calmly replied, "Life is not in your hands but in God's." Those words, spoken in that dramatic moment, were embedded in my heart. They still are.

The Gestapo left. Mother took me in her arms, trying to soothe me. But my aching heart kept repeating, "They've got Papa."

Mother told me: "It wasn't our turn to be led into the Lions' den. Whenever Jehovah allows our arrest, he will give us the needed strength. Let's pray for Dad and for us both, begging our heavenly Father to sustain us." Her prayer was like ointment upon an aching wound.

❧ ❧ ❧

Mother was pale when she came out of the bank. The Gestapo had closed our account. Then she came out empty-handed from the employment office.

"No one can work without a working card," Mother said. I took her hand as she caressed my hair. Hatred flared up in me. They arrested my dad the day he got his monthly pay. They closed our bank account and refused Mum a working card, saying that there was neither work nor help for vermin.

"Mum, what are we going to eat? How are we going to live?" The uncertainty added to my fear in spite of Mum's reassuring words, "Our Father in heaven will not forsake us."

The Koehls responded quickly, supplying our essential needs. Their generosity and help was a real blessing. Mum, in turn, insisted on doing their mending and sewing. I decided to help out wherever I could.

Father, 1939 (photo from identity document)

Mother, 1941, after Dad's arrest

Simone, 1941, age 11

Aunt Eugenie, 1940

I burned with anger at what the Nazis had done to our family. But Mum kept telling me that our enemy was, not the people, but their ideology. Didn't we know that our greatest enemy is Satan? Mum had to say it over and over again.

We missed Dad so much. My playmate and art teacher was gone. No evening kiss, no knees to climb on. Dad was in prison. His vivid Bible reading, his exciting historical accounts, his "trips" on the map—our wonderful evenings together were gone. The armchair was vacant. His place at the table was empty. Every evening, Zita sat in front of Dad's armchair and howled.

"Let's change our furniture around," Mother decided suddenly. She bought an old table and put it in our living room. It had just one leg in the middle. "This will give me more space for my sewing," she said. She took the tabletop off and sawed a few inches off the leg. With plywood she made a shallow box with two open sides and nailed it between the leg and the tabletop, bringing the table back to its original height. "Now we have a secret hiding place for Bible literature."

The news spread rapidly. The Gestapo had begun hunting down Jehovah's Witnesses of Mulhouse. First, a young lad, Paul Dossman, was arrested. A few days later, Eugen Lenz fell into a police trap. They even arrested Mr. Huber, the gray-haired, distinguished grandpa, who was more than 60 years old. We wondered who would be next.

At school, I couldn't concentrate anymore. I worried constantly. Has Mum been arrested? Will the Lion get us today? When I arrived home each afternoon, it was such a relief to find Mum still there! It wasn't our turn today. Maybe tomorrow. The Gestapo clearly intended to destroy Jehovah's Witnesses.

❧ ❧ ❧

As soon as people in town saw Mother and me coming, they stopped talking and quickly separated, as if we were lepers. Only Maria Hartmann, a lady living on our street, had the courage to visit us. She knew more about Dad's arrest than we did. Listening to Maria's account and looking at mother's drawn face, her blue eyes brimming with tears, I got mad all over again. Dad had been arrested at 10:00 a.m. that awful day, right in the factory and in front of his coworkers! The Gestapo had called loudly for Adolphe Arnold, and they asked Dad if he was a Bible Student.

"Come with us!" the Gestapo had demanded. He had to walk in front of them, to the satisfaction of some Nazi supporters who laughed at him. They ordered him to take his bike and pedal in front of the Gestapo car as it headed to our house. Dad had been treated like a common criminal; they had made a public spectacle of him. People had come to the windows to see what was going on.

My anger grew stronger and stronger; nightmares tired me out. In the morning, Mother's eyes were red, her eyelids swollen. But I didn't see her cry, and I swallowed my tears too. I grew more and more numb. Still, each time I heard men's footsteps in our stairway, I grabbed hold of Mum's apron.

Mother went to the prison to pick up Dad's underwear and to take clean clothes to him. She tried to smuggle a Bible in to him. The warden told her secretly: "Don't you dare do this again. We destroy everything, and we also have to report it." Mum knew that it was the death sentence for anyone who got caught smuggling a Bible or Bible literature into the prison. She wondered whether she had been reported to the Gestapo. Each day we waited for them to come.

The Gestapo and the police often arrested people secretly, waiting for the darkness of the night to act. Mum was ready. She had sewn a secret girdle for herself. She put a tiny Bible in the girdle and wore it during the day. At night she kept it next to her in bed.

We tried to stay alert; the slightest noise woke us up. The circles around our eyes got darker and darker. We encouraged each other by praying and reading the Bible together. Mum and I went for a walk. Once more she patiently tried to help me understand that wrong teachings can make humans act like animals.

A man walked toward us. He asked us to step aside to a more concealed place. Mum recognized him. He was our tapestry maker.

"I'm happy to see you again," the man whispered. "You know, I had to give up my business. During wartime, only high German officials can buy new tapestries. I didn't want to work for them. I have a new job as a prison guard."

He told us that Dad was in solitary confinement, that he awoke after hours of unconsciousness in a dark cell, and that he prayed constantly. He was obviously at peace with himself. "The cell is cold and damp. Bring him warm underwear." Before leaving, he said: "Please, when you come to the prison, pretend that you don't know me, all right? I moved your husband to a cell with daylight and brought him the Bible from the prison library."

Mum looked at me, her eyes shining. I knew what she was thinking without her saying a word: "God's hand is not too short. He never abandons us."

We gradually got used to the terrible emptiness caused by Dad's absence. Our mental torment over the prospect of being arrested faded. When the cold weather arrived, we couldn't afford much coal. I sat in my chilly room, looking at the falling snow. I used to love to play in it, but now I wondered how Dad was doing. He had been moved from

Schirmeck camp to the concentration camp in Dachau, along with four other Witnesses from our town. Dad was only allowed to send us a letter of 12 lines, handwritten and censored, every three months.

Just before Dad's arrest, Marcel Sutter had been baptized as a Witness. He replaced Father as the primary teacher for our little group. To prepare the study material, Marcel would come to our home and discuss it with us. In just a few months of intense study, he had come to a very clear understanding of the Bible.

One day, Marcel told Mum that I was much too serious for my age. He suggested that I take piano lessons again. Mother tried to explain that we couldn't afford it. Besides, music didn't seem proper since Dad was in the concentration camp. But Marcel convinced her, insisting that he would pay for my lessons. Every time Marcel came, he would sit in Dad's armchair and listen closely to my piano playing. "Imagine how your father will enjoy your progress," he often said. Little by little, music eased my anguish.

Mum still found people interested in learning about the Bible. The secret visits soon filled all our afternoons. And every evening our hearts were full of thanks to our heavenly Father. We felt deep satisfaction and joy at seeing others grow to love God as we did. They too were ready to face hard times.

All of us—including Marcel Sutter, who was like an older brother, and Adolphe the barber, my second father—waited anxiously for Dad's letters. They strengthened us all. We became a tight-knit family.

One day, Aunt Eugenie asked me to go to Marcel Graf's to help prepare the German translation of the *Watchtower* magazine. The usual reader of the French *Watchtower* was sick. I was to replace him, reading the text out loud as Marcel translated it into German.

Marcel's one-room apartment was on the second floor of the building next to Adolphe's barbershop. The feather bed on the table looked like a bird's nest. The typewriter sat on top of it. Heavy bed covers hung on both windows to dampen our voices. Bertha Graf, Marcel's wife, listened closely for any suspicious noise. If she heard the door creaking downstairs, she would immediately call to her husband; he would run upstairs to the attic while the Koehls and I disappeared into the barber's apartment. Bertha had to take the machine, put it on the bed, and pull the feather bed over it. We became experts at these fast-paced maneuvers.

The single light bulb hanging on a long line gave off a yellowish light and cast eerie shadows in the apartment. The duplicating machine was hardly visible, standing on its wooden box. The Koehls operated the machine. Adolphe turned the crank while Maria handled the paper and the stencils. We were all tense when they worked the machine. If the Gestapo appeared suddenly, there was no

way to hide it. Capture would have meant arrest and even a death sentence.

Once the work was done, the machine had to be taken apart, greased to avoid rusting, and put back into the wooden box. Getting the equipment to and from the hiding place was a dangerous undertaking. It had to be done during the new moon; the city lights were out because of air raids. The courage of Adolphe, Marcel, and their wives was contagious, building our faith and our determination.

We secretly received the latest book, entitled *Children*. It was too big to hide in Mum's table box. It was written in an unusual style—as a dialogue between "John" and "Eunice," a young couple engaged to be married who were Bible Students. We would get to keep the manuscript for an entire week. Every day, we read from it. We called our literature "vitamins," our spiritual food.

❧ ❧ ❧

Heavy boots came stomping upstairs. The blood drained from our faces. The bell rang again and again—long and insistent.

"Gestapo! Open the door!"

The Lion was back. The Gestapo had come many times and had never found our hiding place, but the *Children* book was in the closet among some papers. I disappeared into Mother's room.

"You have forbidden literature in your house!"

Mum said, "Please do your job; the place is yours." She stepped aside. One man hastily entered the living room and went straight to the closet. In the mirror I could see him holding the book, a great smile of satisfaction upon his face.

This is the day of our arrest, I thought. They'll question us about where we got the book. They'll find out the serial number of the typewriter, exposing the Grafs. They'll try all kinds of torture on us. The man turned one page and then several more. Everywhere he found "John: . . . ", "Eunice: . . . " Suddenly he burst out laughing. "Look at that! She reads love stories to replace her husband." He tossed the book back into the closet.

They left grumbling, still convinced that we had some Bible literature hidden somewhere! How could words describe our feelings? Once more we had escaped the Lion's teeth. Not only were we safe but the typewriter had not been found.

❧ ❧ ❧

Our group was diverse. Mr. Berger was an atheist but a defender of religious freedom. His wife, Julie, and her sisters, Helen and Marguerite, were well-known by the neighbors. They attended the meetings, along with a few others. One rainy day, everyone arrived except Adolphe Koehl. We just knew he had been arrested.

I looked around. Everyone sat stiff and tense. Most of those in attendance had just started to study the Bible, but all were ready to stand up for their beliefs. Aware of the gravity of the situation, Mum spoke up. "Perhaps it would be appropriate to pray and to read the Psalms together before we try to depart."

It was late when we heard a soft knock. Julie opened the door. There in the dark stood a man, soaking wet, with his collar pulled up and his dripping hat pulled down low on his brow. He looked just like the secret police investigators. She asked, "What are you looking for?" Our Bibles had gone back in our bags, and somebody had brought herb tea from the stove. The man stepped inside, turning his collar down and taking his hat off. It was Adolphe!

"This will be our last meeting in this location," he told us. "This morning at the barbershop, a customer told me that he had overheard a conversation about a plan to arrest us. A spy was supposed to wait until I entered the house where we meet. So I decided to come a little later than usual. I saw someone standing under the neighbor's balcony. I stopped, and we both stood still for a long time. Then I walked across the road toward him and pointed my big portable light in his face. That way he couldn't see me. Maybe he thought I was a policeman. I walked off, checking in some other corners. When I came back an hour later, he was gone."

❧ ❧ ❧

We felt like we were sinking deeper and deeper in a dangerous mire. On special days, the swastika flag had to be hung from each apartment window. But the apartment next to ours had a window on our street side. So no one noticed that we didn't display the swastika.

Victory after victory by the German army confirmed in the minds of many the motto "God is with us" that the soldiers had inscribed on their belt buckles. Radio reports never mentioned German defeats.

There were shortages of food, wares, and coal. Even cats and dogs became rare. People turned paved courtyards into vegetable gardens. Farmers came under drastic control. They had to turn over all their milk to the Germans. If someone cheated by watering down the milk, he had a big sign painted on his house, "I'm a thief of the *Volksgemeinschaft*."* The prices rose out of reach of poor workers.

---

*This typical Nazi term is a combination of the German words "*Volk*," literally meaning "people" or "nation," and "*Gemeinschaft*," meaning "community." According to Nazi usage, *Volk* became associated with notions of Aryan racial unity, purity, and superiority. A pure-blooded master race was to be the common goal. Each member of the *Volksgemeinschaft* had an equal and solemn responsibility to defend the oneness and greatness of the German nation.

Mother gathered wild greens, such as dandelions and nettles. She soaked old bread in water and then baked it again. It was crunchy and smelled delicious. We slept in a cold room, but Mum put some warm bricks in our bed. To save wood and coal, she wrapped a coal briquette in wet newspaper. If we burned it in the stove at 9:00 p.m., we would find a few embers in the morning, ready to be revived.

Mum never complained. She was just so thankful for what we had and loved to remind me that we didn't feel the despair that most people did. And if we were suffering, at least we knew why. She spoke with pride about Dad's faithfulness and about how he wore the purple triangle identifying him as one of Jehovah's Witnesses. After several months in Dachau, he was allowed to receive one parcel a month. But how could we keep sending food in such hard times? Somehow she managed. Every month Dad received a liter of fish oil, which was not rationed. And no one would be tempted to steal it. Besides, it was healthy for him.

Mum was also able to get some spice-bread cookies. She copied some words from *The Watchtower* onto thin parchment paper, rolled it like a tiny little cigarette, and put it between two cookies that she glued together with some ersatz honey. How dangerous that was! And we had to wait so long to know if it worked. Finally, one day Dad wrote and thanked us for his parcel and the "vitamins"!

CHAPTER 6

Alone Before the Lion

SEPTEMBER 1942

The Parish priest came to our class for weekly catechism. As he entered, he said, "Heil Hitler!" The class stood up and answered, "Heil Hitler, amen!"* Three other girls stepped outside with me to wait until the hour was over. In the courtyard a large tree gave us the needed shelter and a trunk to lean on. We reviewed our school lessons.

We were not aware that a teacher had gone by. When she reached the door, she turned around and called us into the hallway, lining us up in front of her. An icy chill ran down my spine, and I stiffened with fright. With an outstretched arm, she shouted, "Heil Hitler!" Only one girl responded.

"What is this?" She saluted again. This time, three girls replied. The teacher swiftly reached out and grabbed my hair, pulled me in front of the others, and saluted again. Once more the three girls replied. The teacher looked at me with fire in her eyes. "Obviously you do not want to salute. WHY?"

"I can't!"

"And why not?"

"The Heil belongs to Jesus Christ. The New Testament says 'there is no other name under the heaven.'"

"You'll hear from us!" Then she spun on her heel and stomped away.

That evening Mum gave me one of her precious lessons. She knew that this incident was only the beginning. "Whenever you have to face a mean person, stay calm, be polite, and look into the person's eyes. But in your

---

*The bishop of Freiburg, in a pastoral letter, directed the priests to make the Hitler salute mandatory in catechism classes.

mind, fix your heart upon Jehovah, Jesus, and the angels. Imagine their approving smile each time you stand up for what is right."

The following day was Saturday. The principal, Mr. Gasser, had called for me, and I knocked timidly at his door. I heard "Come in," followed by "Heil Hitler." I stood motionless in the doorway.

"Come over here. I'll read you a note from the city supervisor: 'The student Simone Arnold refuses to salute. It is your duty to break her resistance or dismiss her from school.'" A long silence followed. Mr. Gasser stood up. He had an imposing stature.

"Why do you refuse?"

I looked straight into his eyes. "Because I'm a Christian."

His forehead wrinkled up with surprise, and he said, "So am I."

He continued: "But you can't stay in our school unless you salute. If you refuse, you'll become an outcast, and all your abilities and potential will be useless. Try to understand that, and don't make a foolish decision."

That evening Mother's warm voice once again brought to life the story from the book of Daniel, the one about the three Hebrews. The golden image, the music, the wrath of Nebuchadnezzar—I was right in the scene. Mother's calm voice reflected the courage of the three young men when they stood erect while everybody else bowed down to the image. They feared, not men, or even death by fire, but God. And an angel rescued them. In the peaceful moonlight of that night, I finally fell asleep.

"Child, you have made your own decision—a wise one. You have to stick to your decision to be at peace with yourself. Remember how often your dad used to say to you, 'Listen to the voice of your conscience.' Recall the three Hebrews. Never forget that their God is our God too. He is almighty, and he will give you strength."

Yes, I had refused. I could have given in, but I knew that Jehovah's eyes were upon me.

❧ ❧ ❧

I was almost late for school. Once I was seated, Mr. Zipf put his hand upon my shoulder. He seemed troubled. Why? A knock at the door brought the answer. A boy came in with a circular. It stated: "It has come to our attention that a student is refusing to comply with civic duties. Every student must comply. No exceptions will be tolerated. This is the last warning. 'Heil Hitler!'"

After a while, Mr. Zipf discreetly called me. He pointed out a sentence at the bottom of the circular. It read, "This circular is to be presented to all classes by Simone Arnold."

"I'm sorry, I can't go against this, Simone. You'll have to go to all the classes and return the paper to me. Each teacher must read it out loud and then sign it."

I started to tremble. My legs felt like lead. How could I enter each class without saying 'Heil Hitler'?

The more I delayed, the more anxious I became. I slowly approached the door of the first classroom. Timidly, I knocked. "Come in." I wanted to run away, but my feet were glued to the floor. The heads of all the children turned around. I couldn't speak. The teacher called me over and quickly scanned the paper. Glaring at the class, she started reading aloud, stressing each word. Then she signed the paper and concluded the same way she had begun, with a loud "Heil Hitler." Dragging myself, I left the classroom downhearted.

I knocked at the next classroom. Again I stood motionless at the entrance. After glancing at my trembling paper, the teacher ordered, "Close the door behind you and stay where you are." Addressing the class, he said: "Pay close attention. We have a letter from the supervisor." He read some sentences twice, and then he stepped out through a side door. When he came back, every one of the more than 40 children stood up and shouted, "Heil Hitler!" The teacher handed back the circular, pointed to the door, and dismissed me—just the way Grandma did her dog! I felt so humiliated.

I came back to my class with just two signatures. "You'd better get at least two more for today," Mr. Zipf suggested. "You've got a long way to go to get through all 24 classes!" I felt like running away.

When I got back to my class, Mr. Zipf whispered, "Tomorrow, you'll have to continue."

As I walked home, my conscience was stinging me. I felt that I shouldn't have panicked. I shouldn't be terrified about going back to school. At dinner, the meal sat on my plate; I couldn't eat or talk. Mother didn't press me, but she could sense that I was deeply upset about something. I finally told her what had happened.

In bed, I cuddled in Mum's arms, trying to warm myself and get rid of the chills. Mum reassured me that the fear I had felt was only normal and that it did not mean that I lacked faith. In her prayer that night, she thanked Jehovah for her courageous daughter. A warm, peaceful feeling made me curl up comfortably, and soon I was sound asleep.

At breakfast the next morning, Mum said, "Simonette, if you want to stay home, I'll write a note and take it to school." But I had decided to let all the teachers know that I was not ashamed of my decision. I would show them all that I wouldn't heil a man.

Mr. Zipf looked at me. I went up and asked if I could continue right away visiting the other classes. It would be best to get it over with as quickly as possible. It was better not to listen to the reading, not to look at all the faces. I remembered that it was a privilege to stand as a Witness of Jehovah. I had done nothing wrong.

It was going to be a whole week with the same pressure. But I remembered: Didn't Mum pray to Jehovah to help me? In each class, while the teacher read the circular, I picked out something in the classroom to focus on in order to ease the pressure. I was determined to follow through, and I did so with growing confidence. But throughout that week, my teacher, Mr. Zipf, grew increasingly nervous. His hands shook as he gave me an envelope. "Give this to your mother, and bring me her written answer tomorrow." It was an invitation to tea at his home. The next day I brought him Mum's reply.

It was a bright Thursday afternoon, but inside Mr. Zipf's home, it was dark and dismal. All the shutters and the heavy velvet curtains were closed. Mr. Zipf seemed happy that we had accepted his invitation. His wife poured the tea and left us alone.

With concern in his voice, Mr. Zipf said: "Since the day Simone started to go to the 24 classes with that circular, I've been agitated and unable to sleep. I do not want to lose such a pleasant, hard-working student." He said that we didn't know what we were heading for and that he was afraid of how things might turn out.

Mr. Zipf continued: "We owe a lot to Hitler. It's true that he demands unconditional obedience. But after all, doesn't he deserve honor and thanks for what he has done for our nation? You well know the humiliating situation Germany was in. Hitler gave us bread; he gave us money; he restored our honor. Great Germany will be the protector of Christian values against godless Communism. Maybe the Führer is the envoy of God. I consider it my duty to let you know how harmful your stand is. I'm a Christian too, and I sometimes teach at the Baptist church. I know the Bible well. You have been misled." A lively Bible discussion followed between Mr. Zipf and Mum.

I was surprised at the things Mr. Zipf said. He quoted Jesus' words 'give Caesar's things to Caesar' and said that God doesn't want Christians to suffer. Christians should obey the government so that they could continue to preach. It is better to be alive and preach than to be in prison or even dead.

Mother's reply puzzled me at first: "Mr. Zipf, when the apostles said, 'We must obey God as ruler rather than men,' don't their words indicate that men in power can encroach upon the law of the Most High? What do you think the apostle's words meant?"

"You can't take the Bible literally. You have to get the spirit of it. God is merciful—he knows we are weak and can't apply all his laws. He forgives. But now I would like to talk to Simone. She can make her own decision."

He invited me to sit closer. Again he told me how much he liked me. He said that he didn't want to see my whole life ruined. "Simone, you have read Jesus' words, 'Be cautious like a serpent and innocent like a dove.' That's the way a Christian has to be. As a Christian, I also do not agree with the 'Heil Hitler' salute.

"I'll tell you what you should do," he continued.

"Follow my example. I do not heil either. Haven't you noticed that I never lift my right arm, the arm I swear with? That arm is for God. I lift the left one, and in my heart I pray for forgiveness. I'm just cautious like the serpent. Simone, God does not want you to destroy your future and maybe even your life. God forgives our sins. He is like a father—fathers forgive."

"I can't do that."

"And why not?"

"Because that would be compromising. If someone found out what I was doing, I'd be viewed as a liar. I do not want to be taken for a liar."

Mr. Zipf blushed slightly. "Simone, you worry too much about doing what's right. You still have another full day to finish visiting the classes. Think about our conversation, and remember—a Christian has to be cautious like a serpent. A serpent doesn't willingly confront its enemy. Whenever it can, it sneaks away."

The following school day, Friday, I went to pick up the paper to take to the last classes on the list. Mr. Zipf looked at me, disappointment on his face. "Simone, please remember, be cautious like the serpent!"

Saturday, Mr. Zipf was missing. The handwriting on the blackboard assigned us some work to do. The class was silent except for the sound of the scratching of ink pens on paper and the turning of pages. My friends Anita and Daniele hadn't come back to school during my whole week of suffering. Why didn't Mr. Zipf come this morning? For more than an hour, we did our schoolwork without any teacher present. I felt uneasy.

Suddenly the door flew open. My classmates stood erect, raised their arms, and responded as one: "Heil Hitler!" As usual, I stood up but kept my arm down. Mr. Zipf searched for my arm and shot a desperate look at me. Two other men entered the classroom. Mr. Gasser, the principal, stood opposite the big desk where the other man, the city supervisor, had taken a seat. The city supervisor spoke with power and authority, glorifying Germany's government. He praised Hitler as the protector of our heritage, defender of the German race, provider of a secure future for the thousand years to come.

He then mentioned that a teacher had brought to his attention that one student was refusing to fulfill her duty. "I have given this student a whole week to decide, and the time is now up. In Germany, each one is free to choose his fate or destiny because we love freedom! It is your class that has the rebellious student who refuses to do her duty."

A murmur rippled through the class. The city supervisor scrutinized the faces, looking for the one turning red with embarrassment. His eyes skipped over me. But Mr. Zipf and Mr. Gasser gazed at me. My hands were cold; my heart started beating faster.

The city supervisor continued his ranting speech. "This school cannot keep a student who refuses to honor our Führer. The 'Heil Hitler' salute is an obligation. No one can remain free from punishment if that one refuses to salute. Does the student wish to identify herself as one who voluntarily refuses to salute?"

A long silence followed. Mr. Zipf's eyes begged, "Stand up and salute just once; be cautious like a serpent." Now my heart was really pounding.

"If the student refuses to heil Hitler, let her identify herself by standing up." I stood up and looked straight at him. A roaring noise came over the class. I could feel Mr. Zipf's nervousness. He looked down at his feet and shifted his weight from one to the other, while Mr. Gasser gritted his teeth. The city supervisor's eyes darkened. He looked just like Hitler, whose picture hung above the blackboard. He shouted, "Simone Arnold, come up here!" He pushed me toward the blackboard.

"Face the class!" I faced the class. My head was pounding.

"You are ruining your life; you alone bear the responsibility!" he screamed. "If you don't salute, here are your papers, your dismissal. But since it is a decision for life, I am giving you one last chance to make the right choice. I shall give you five more minutes." He pulled back his left sleeve to check his watch. "After five minutes either you say 'Heil Hitler' in front of his picture or you take your dismissal and leave!"

Five minutes can seem an eternity! A hush came over the whole class. I felt all those eyes looking at me—the piercing eyes of the city supervisor and the pleading eyes of the two teachers on my left. In front of me, more than 40 students stared, some with fear or curiosity, but some with scorn, even with hatred. And Hitler's dreadful eyes—the ones I had seen more than two years before—now seemed to be staring out at me from the frame.

I felt that my head would explode any minute. Only one thought was solidly fixed in my mind. It became a voice, a very strong voice, telling me, "You have to take

those dismissal papers—the papers, they're what you want—the papers."

The supervisor checked his watch. His arm shot up, "Heil Hitler!" His shrieking voice jolted the other two teachers. The whole class responded immediately, amplifying as with one voice the shrill sound of the salute. I held my breath. I felt the blood, which had flushed my face, suddenly leaving. I snatched the papers, clutched them tight to my heart, and ran out of class.

I stopped under the shade of the same tree where my troubles had begun. What a delightful feeling came over me! I felt that I had pleased God. I wanted to shout for joy.

A sudden realization momentarily dampened my joy. In the *Volksschule,* I wouldn't be able to continue my studies. Biology, physics, chemistry—none of these were available. But I was sure of God's approval—that was the greatest treasure. I felt drawn to him. He had given me a victory over the Nazi Lion.

Suddenly, I felt a familiar hand upon my shoulder. A cold shiver went through me when I heard the words: "You cannot just leave school like that. You have to go back to class." Mr. Zipf picked up my schoolbag, which I had laid at the bulging root of the tree.

I hesitated. I could still run to freedom! But what use would it be now to run away? Dragging my feet, I followed Mr. Zipf back to the classroom. The two other men were gone. Standing in front of the class, Mr. Zipf again hailed Germany as a land of freedom, saying that I had been given the freedom to make my own choice. With sadness in his voice, he added, "Simone Arnold has chosen to leave this school. We all feel sorry about her choice. We'll miss her. She has been a good student, and we love her." Then he sat down. He swallowed hard and drew a deep breath. His emotion brought tears to my eyes—the only tears I shed in this school.

Mother was overjoyed. Marcel excitedly congratulated me. Adolphe's eyes beamed, conveying his approval. I thought how proud my father would be. And most of all, I knew my faithfulness had made the heavens rejoice. But in my heart, the seeds of self-satisfaction and pride started to grow. The humiliation of having to return to the *Volksschule* drove my pride inward, hidden deep in my heart.

❧ ❧ ❧

Mum came along to have me registered in my old school again, and I was glad she came. We knocked at the door of Mr. Ehrlich, the principal.

When Mr. Ehrlich realized that we had come in without giving the Hitler salute, he jumped up and snarled, "Arnold, you are the Arnolds!" Lifting a paper over his head, he circled his desk and then slammed the paper down. Pacing back and forth, he screamed: "Do you really believe that I'll take a rebellious child in my school? A child who challenges school discipline has no place here. Just who do you think you are?"

Mum's calm and firm voice seemed to upset him even more. His head bobbed up and down as he spat out insults and accusations. Not only did he use foul words but also his breath stank horribly and he sprayed us with saliva.

Finally Mother was able to speak. "My daughter has never been 'a rebellious child' during all the time she was in the *Mittelschule.* For your information, no one ever filed a complaint against her for misbehavior. But if you believe you can't take Simone, then please sign a statement to that effect, and I'll keep her home. I can teach her myself!"

He flopped down in his chair stammering, "I can't. I have no right. No—no...."

Mother took the opportunity to offer a suggestion: "Simone can make a solemn promise that she will always be polite and discreet and will never cause a disturbance."

His face changed. Obviously he had an idea. "I'll give you a chance but on the condition that no one is to know why you were dismissed from the *Mittelschule*. You are under prohibition. Don't you dare tell!"

Mum concluded that it was an acceptable proposal. What a relief that was for me! Mother was rudely dismissed, leaving me with the grumbling principal. He nervously scratched out a note and placed it in a sealed envelope. I had to go upstairs to Miss Lorenz's class with the message. I tried to read the writing through the thin envelope. The few words I could read told me that I was to be left out, pushed aside. My heart was pounding as I entered the classroom. I was startled to see all the students facing me. The door was just next to the blackboard. It was a big class.

Miss Lorenz let me stand near her desk, and once more I felt all those searching eyes upon me. Then she opened the envelope. Her eyes widened with astonishment. She ordered a girl sitting in the last row to move to another place and sent me to the vacant seat. I spotted Andrée, Blanche, and Madeleine. I was so relieved that at least I had some friends here.

The teacher didn't introduce me, but quite a few of the children remembered me. The dismissal bell rang, and the children came over and wanted to know why I had left *Mittelschule*. They were completely unsatisfied when I said, "I can't tell you—it's a secret." Day after day they picked on me. They were sure that I had misbehaved, stolen, or lied. They said I had been sent off because I was lazy. My denials without explanation only made things worse. Their malicious backbiting became a game. My three friends never participated, yet they avoided me. The teacher wouldn't calm the jeering children during playtime.

I suffered the deepest humiliation when the kids hollered: "You don't have the courage to tell us. You are a ...

coward ... coward ... coward; that's what you are." They accused me of being weak and worthless. Me—accusing me! I had been faithful to my vow and had stood up for my beliefs.

A terrible conflict raged in my heart. I was afraid to tell Mum about it. It had been easier to face all the classes with the circular than to keep silent in front of the ridicule and lies. I stuck to my promise to keep my mouth shut, but I was rebelling in my heart.

Each day, Mum saw that I left for school at the very last minute and returned home immediately after school let out. She figured out what was wrong. Mum and Adolphe repeatedly reminded me that I shouldn't pay attention to what people said. Every situation has a lesson, they told me. But it was not easy for me to draw the line between self-respect and pride, between humility and weakness, between outside appearance and inner qualities. However, their repeated encouragement gave me the strength to face up to the verbal assaults.

My reading of Mr. Ehrlich's note had been correct—I was to have no books, and I was not allowed to read or participate. The classes in this school were far behind the teaching of *Mittelschule*. At least Marcel Sutter had tutored me well in mathematics. And I was sure that in the future, under Messiah's peaceful rule, I would have plenty of time to catch up and go back to advanced learning. But this ban on my participation in class was surely meant to crush my spirit.

In class, I copied from my classmate Ginette's book and illustrated each page of my notebook with some drawings. I had nothing in common with Ginette. She was tall; I was small. She was outspoken; I was reserved. She loved to be the center of a group; I preferred private conversations. But she never joined in the ridicule. She served as a screen. It was easy for me, the tiny one, to hide behind that tall pole.

On the other hand, I disliked Ginette's curiosity. I felt her eyes constantly looking over my shoulder. Whenever possible I avoided giving her any information. However, her irritating curiosity eased my dilemma. One day when the teacher was out, she tried again to find out why I had such a strange attitude. Some children thought I was proud and high-minded. But she had come up with another reason.

Ginette was sure that she knew the answer to my riddle. "You were expelled because you do not salute, and you never sing patriotic songs. I watch you! You can't hide anything from me. You're in the French Resistance!"

This was more than I could take! Now I had to tell the reason! I just couldn't let her think I was a French resister, involved in some political movement.

"I was sent off because I'm a Christian!"

"So am I."

"If you were, you wouldn't heil Hitler!"

"And why not?"

"The Bible says that there is only one name under heaven by which we can be saved. 'Heil' means salvation, and salvation only comes through Jesus!" Ginette did not realize that she had opened the cell in which I had been held a prisoner. Now I was free to talk!

My schoolbag wouldn't fit into my desk. Ginette leaned over and said, "Don't force it. There is a parcel in there for your Dad. Take it home. Hide it in your jacket." At home I spread the contents out on the table. I was overjoyed! Flour, butter, sugar, jam—just what we needed to bake a nice cake for Dad. But what a disappointment when Mother told me to put everything back in the box and to find out where Ginette lived!

"But Mum, this is not for us. It's for Dad. We have to send it to Dad."

"We do not need strangers to send Dad a parcel. We don't know why they've done this. It could be stolen merchandise or just a trap."

We headed for Ginette's house to return Dad's parcel. The day was so hot! The sun burned our heads as we walked down the long street with barely any shade. I grumbled about the sun, about the long way, about everything.

Ginette's mother, a tall, thin lady, seemed a bit nervous as she invited us in. "I knew you would come to bring the parcel back." She wanted to meet us both, and she added, "People like you have to be brought back to the Catholic Church!"

I was startled when Mum told her that it would be possible for us to return to the Church—if she would prove the basis of her faith with scriptures from the Bible. "But," Mum said, "be honest, and let the Bible speak. I also have to warn you about the danger of our visit. You may be exposed to persecution." While both mothers had a lively discussion, I had the same with Ginette. She and her mom were both eager to learn. This was the start of a regular Bible discussion.

Mum later told me, "Just think, you had to be put out of *Mittelschule* and be seated near Ginette. It must have been an angel who got Miss Lorenz to seat you next to her! Helping our neighbors to build their faith is worth everything."

❧ ❧ ❧

LATE 1942

It was our second winter without Dad. With even less coal than the year before, it was harder than ever. Outside, the icy wind tried to get in through even the smallest opening. The morning breeze howled in the cold chimney, proclaiming another frigid day. By dawn the fireplace would have just a few embers left, and our shutters would be frozen shut again. The windows could not be opened without a hot iron to melt the ice.

Life wasn't easy for anybody, but without any income and with the constant threat of arrest, we had added burdens to bear. The anguish of not knowing Dad's fate was an even heavier load. Alsace was now German. While "undesirables" languished in German concentration camps, others tried to flee to southern France, and the ones still at home had to submit to German rule.

Gauleiter Wagner, Hitler's personal agent, intensified the *Heim in's Reich*—going back home (to Germany)—program. The Nazi youth group for girls, as well as the Hitler Youth group, had been established. The *Reichsarbeitsdienst* demanded that 18-year-old girls give one year of service to the State. There was talk about starting up the draft. Listening to foreign radio could result in severe punishment.

Each apartment house had at least one spy, and some even had a spy to spy on the spy! All sorts of resisters were arrested, as were all kinds of ordinary people who were turned in and denounced simply out of hate or jealousy.

Grandma feared for her deaf son, Germain. She had learned that the Nazis were conducting T-4, the so-called euthanasia program, to eliminate people with mental or physical defects.

The sudden disappearance of "undesirable" people gave me new nightmares. Would they come and get us too? Mum had packed a suitcase with a Bible, rice, sugar, and woolens. It stood like a menace, reminding us of our precarious situation. They took Brother Schaguené, his wife, and his son away. Next was Brother Schoenauer, who had already lost his job with the railroad because he wouldn't join the Nazi programs.

All civilians had to support the war effort. They had to knit stockings, gloves, and earmuffs for the soldiers. Children had to go from door to door to collect old paper, bones, cans, and scrap iron. Every week, each student had to bring six pounds of material to school, and the amount was recorded. I had not collected any. Now I again had to decide for myself what to do. The notebook had no entries for me, but Miss Lorenz didn't say a thing. Most students brought more than required, and the pile under the covered courtyard grew.

❧ ❧ ❧

MARCH 1943

Mum received an order to bring me to Sinne Street, next to the theater. A psychiatrist was to give me a mental evaluation. I wondered why I had to have such a test. Were they going to do something to my brain? Mum prayed with me and then took me to the office.

The waiting room was gloomy. Some people sat there on benches. When Mum noticed who was there, she put her finger to her lips, indicating that we should keep silent. The three Arzt boys, who had recently become Jehovah's Witnesses, were there, as well as Jeanette, the eight-year-old daughter of Fritz Lauber. He was a widower, a German army veteran of World War I. He had a wooden leg, and they had taken his pension away because he was a Bible Student. We children had all refused to heil Hitler. Mum thought it would be best if we pretended that we did not know one another.

Suddenly the door opened, and a harsh voice called "Lauber." The visit was short. With a reassuring nod, Fritz let us know that everything had gone well. The Arzt boys were called next. I was the last one, but we had to wait quite a while.

We entered the whitewashed room. Straight ahead was a window looking out at the park. To our left was an L-shaped table. The two doctors wore white coats. One, a small man, checked a huge notebook. The second one was taller and had a round face. In the middle of the room sat an empty chair with its back to the park. I was ordered to sit there. I faced a big round interrogation light. Mum sat in another chair behind me.

The taller man got up, turned on the light, and pointed it at my face. I could hardly see the two men anymore, and I found it very difficult to apply what Mum had told me: "Never look down. Always look straight ahead, eye to eye." The light was just too bright.

The doctor sat down and asked my name. Mother started to answer. "Shut up!" he shouted. "We're talking to your daughter. We don't want to hear a word from you!" The setting seemed familiar somehow. Their harsh voices brought September 4, 1941, back to my mind. That was the day my father was arrested and Mum spent nearly four hours under the Gestapo's cross-examination.

“This is going to be an IQ test,” said the doctor seated to my right. Then, in lightning fashion, the two doctors began firing questions at the same time.

“Give me the five continents starting with the smallest,” said one. I hadn’t answered yet when another question came from my left.

“You have meetings—yes or no?”

“The five continents. Quickly!”

“The meetings.”

“No, we can’t have meetings,” I finally answered. “The French banned us.”

“Name the five longest European rivers.”

“You have the *Watchtower* magazine—yes or no?”

“The five rivers…”

“Yes or no?”

The shorter man constantly snapped his fingers to speed up my answers. He came back to some questions over and over again.

“But we know you print *The Watchtower*—yes or no?” “No,” I answered. As far as I was concerned, typing wasn’t printing.

“What is three times 97?”

"Where does *The Watchtower* come from?"

"How did you come up with the answer 291?"

"Quickly, we have no time! We know that you go to secret meetings—yes or no?"

"No." For me a "meeting" was in an auditorium. Our "family get-together" wasn't public.

"We know you produce books. You can't fool us; you'd better talk."

An hour had gone by. I was foggy, confused. All those questions started to make my head spin. Only one thought was clear in my mind: "Never betray."

I was on the verge of breaking down when suddenly the telephone rang. The men consulted together then got up and left. After a while, another man came and sent us off.

The cool spring air outside helped to revive us; both of us had headaches and were exhausted. Again we had escaped the Lion's attack. How comforted I was to hear Mum say, "You are a courageous girl, and you didn't betray our underground activities." I knew Jehovah had listened to Mum's prayers.

"Mum, if you hadn't prayed for me, I would have been lost because I couldn't pray. They gave me no time."

Mum said: "If Jehovah sees in your heart the firm determination to keep faithful to him, he will give you the means to do it no matter the circumstances. No one can stand up by himself. Always remember that." Her wise words went down deep into my heart.

Courthouse

❧ ❧ ❧

When I came home from school one day, I found Zita lying on a cushion in the corner. She whimpered in pain and struggled to get up but couldn't. I knelt down and lifted her head. Her eyes looked desperate. After a few minutes, she stretched out and died. I ran and locked myself in my room. I couldn't stop crying.

Now the Gestapo could come—Zita was gone! I was sure that someone had poisoned her. Zita's death was accompanied by a summons to court.

At home, we said a prayer and then set off for court. Six months had elapsed since I had been expelled from *Mittelschule*. The old-style courthouse looked like a medieval castle. All around its turrets, stout gargoyles with their terrifying dragon mouths spouted the collected rainwater.

I was determined to defend my beliefs, but as we entered the building, my courage began to wane. Holding the summons in her hands, Mum read the sign on each door, looking for the name of the judge. Once we found the room, Mother uttered a short prayer: "Jehovah, please give us wisdom and strength."

A heavy man with gray hair was expecting us. For several long moments he gazed at me over the top of his glasses before asking if I was Simone Arnold. Then he told us to sit down in front of him. He told Mother not to speak. She could only listen. He said he had to find out if I still persisted in my refusal to heil Hitler.

He wanted to know who had told me to refuse to do civilian duty. When I said, "the Bible," he abruptly looked up.

"And how's that?"

"The Bible says that there is only one name under the heavens by which we shall get saved, and that is Jesus."

With an exceptionally calm voice, he tried to make me believe that Hitler would be the Savior. He would establish a paradise for a thousand years! My future was assured. I could get the best schooling, have a successful career, and enjoy fine living facilities.

In response to my second no, he said: "Why are you so stubborn? Don't you understand where this obstinate decision of yours will lead? Look at your father. Where is he now? It is his teaching that got you into this mess. There is still time to change your mind. You are a good student. Heil Hitler, and you can immediately go back to *Mittelschule!*"

After my third no, his voice changed.

"You force me to order a condemnation—do you understand what that means for you? Instead of climbing up the social ladder, it will be downhill with you!"

"It doesn't matter," I answered. "I want to be approved by God."

"You foolish child. You don't understand what the end will be for you!"

He looked at Mother and said: "What have you done to your child? What a waste! I can't help you. I have to sign the statement pronouncing that she is a victim of the Bible Students. The Gestapo is after you. We have done all we can to avoid this outcome. We work for the *Volksgemeinschaft*, but we have to separate the ones who are rebellious. You bear full responsibility for your child's mental corruption."

He made me sign the statement. It said that I had been told the consequences of my decision and that I continued to claim to be a Bible Student, knowing that the organization was under ban. With a mixture of disappointment and bitterness, he said: "No one can swim against the stream! Swimming against the State means you will drown! You'll see!"

Adolphe had good news for us. One of his clients worked for the *Jugendamt,* the official court for minors. His office had received the documents from the judge, sentencing me to a Nazi reeducational home. But Adolphe's client promised to put the order under a big pile of pending documents. He told Adolphe, "Maybe the Russians will end the war before Simone's order comes up."

Little by little, my school situation became routine. My classmates just ignored me. I could sense that Miss Lorenz didn't share Mr. Ehrlich's opinion; sometimes it showed in her eyes. She even gave me personal training in gymnastics. I was selected for a city youth gymnastic competition. At least I now had the teacher's attention and got to learn something different.

Hundreds of girls and boys from all the area schools had been selected. They wore black shorts and white sleeveless shirts. We had been given a special ticket to buy white gym shoes. Over and over again, we practiced the movements in perfect synchronization with the rousing music. I was completely carried away with the harmonious beauty.

LATE APRIL 1943

The day of our last rehearsal arrived. During the final practice, workers set up poles, hoisted flags, and hung big swastikas. Garlands surrounded the official seats under a huge emblem of an eagle. My concentration was broken by all the Nazi ornamentation. As the parade ground took shape, I started to make mistakes. I was relieved when the practice was over.

I couldn't help but wonder: 'Why hadn't my Mum, Marcel, and Adolphe warned me?' It would have been much easier had they told me: "Don't accept because it's going to be a gathering to glorify Nazism."

The following morning, I told Mum that I had decided not to participate. I was convinced that a Christian couldn't stay amid youth that would heil Hitler. Being one of the smallest, I stood in the front row. How could I stand there without lifting my arm? Mum seemed relieved. She said that had I given it more careful thought, I would have refused even to be trained for it.

"Why didn't you tell me?" I asked indignantly.

"My dear child, it is your conscience that must decide, not somebody else's."

I realized that there was nothing wrong with sports or the theater. But everything about this competition was highly nationalistic. The swastika was everywhere. I definitely did not belong there.

On top of everything, I faced new pressures at school. Mr. Ehrlich had come to our class, telling us that we had been selected to go to a youth camp for two weeks after Pentecost. In the meantime, each child was required to bring 50 pfennig every Monday to the teacher. I didn't say anything to Mum about it.

❧ ❧ ❧

Mother started to teach me more about housework and sewing. "It's better for you to learn from me rather than from strangers." Why did I need to learn? After all, the Gestapo had told us they would take us both away. We would be together; I would do the hard work, and Mum could sew and mend. But Mum insisted.

I enjoyed cooking and liked to show off my skills to Marcel. Mother had gone out, taking care of someone who was in need. Alone at home and expecting the visit of my beloved brother, I suddenly decided to demonstrate my pastry art. I used six eggs and baked a lot of cookies. The smell filled the house. I was so happy when Marcel came in and said that he was proud to have a little sister who could bake such delicious cookies. One cookie after another disappeared.

When Mum came home, there was hardly a cookie left! As soon as Marcel had gone, Mum said, "Poor lad, he must be terribly hungry." Later, she realized that our monthly ration was gone: no butter, no eggs, no sugar.

Mother took me into her arms and told me something that stabbed like a sword in my heart. "Don't worry, we will find something to eat. Marcel enjoyed them, and this will give him a lift. Soon they will start drafting young men. Marcel will be called up, and as a Christian, he will refuse to kill. His refusal will mean death."

I knew that the first Christians were persecuted and some were even killed. Witnesses were dying in concentration camps. But Marcel, my brother—how could he be killed because he refuses to kill? Just thinking about it made me weep. I buried myself under my bedcover, hoping somehow that he wouldn't be drafted.

❧ ❧ ❧

Marcel's remarkable composure strengthened me to face the hardships that lay ahead. Together we talked about our hope of seeing the earth turn into a peaceful garden. We pictured a wonderful future despite the fact that the present looked so uncertain. He brought me a poetry book in which he wrote: "Hope is the greatest treasure. If a man has lost everything, he still possesses hope!" Our common faith and our mutual love for God nourished our hope in the Messianic Kingdom. My heart got attached to his heart, and I looked up to him with deep admiration.

Mother too was as solid as a rock. Her smile, her positive outlook, and her joy of life made me determined to stand up for Christian principles. Her strength not only calmed me but also encouraged those in our brotherhood.

Marcel Sutter, 1942

The scent of lilacs drifted over the countryside and the twitter of birds filled the air—summer wasn't far off. Adolphe Koehl's client had been ordered to work on my case. He had come under police control. He promised to do what he could, but he had limited authority. He would try to delay my departure some more.

Sadly, Marcel's departure was not postponed. He received his draft notice and came to say good-bye. He was fully prepared to face the Lion—the hungry, terrifying beast. Marcel sat in our parlor for the last time. He was calm and serene. He trusted totally in Jehovah. He said he would never kill a person or support any war effort, not even as a civilian in a weapons factory. He was ready to give his own life if necessary.

We prayed intensely together. We fought to hold back the tears. Muffled sobs came out of my throat. Marcel gave me a warm hug and said, "Don't worry." His determined steps as he walked down the street became a living part of my memory. At the corner, he turned around, and we

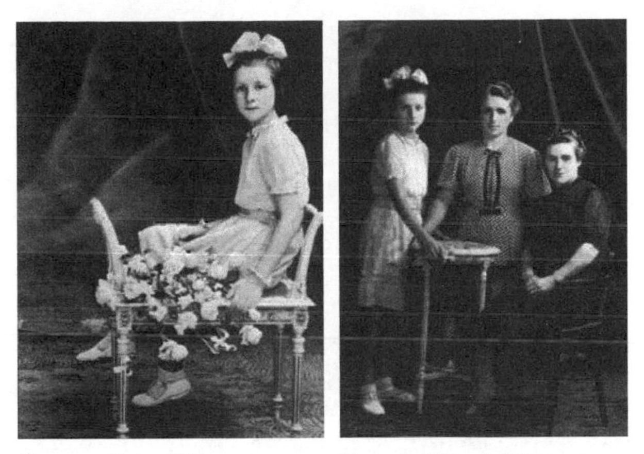

Simone, age 12, June 1943

Simone, Aunt Eugenie, Mother

saw his handsome face for what we knew would be the last time—that is, until it pleases God to reunite us all.

Marcel was taken less than two years after Dad's arrest. Would I be next? I hoped so. Maybe if I was the next one, Mum could stay home. And maybe the war would be over before they came for her!

❧ ❧ ❧

My dear Mum thought that I deserved to have a new dress. She had a bit of pink organza with some airy lilacs, one of Dad's designs. She thought that it would be nice to have a picture taken as a keepsake.

On the appointed day, Aunt Eugenie came along. The photographer arranged a setting with artificial roses. I was to sit and hold the seat with my left hand to show the gloves Aunt Eugenie had crocheted for me. The only thing missing was a new pair of shoes, but we couldn't buy any.

The photographer disappeared behind his huge box and draped a big black cover over himself, leaving just one hand outside, way up over his head. Click! "Another one just in case." Click! "And now what about a family picture?"

He sat Mother next to a dainty table. My aunt stood behind it, and I stood to her right. But that picture made me sad. My beloved father was missing. The photographer kept saying, "Don't make a face like you're attending a funeral!"

Our class planned to go to the youth camp the day after Pentecost. The Friday before, Mr. Ehrlich came to the class. Miss Lorenz handed him the list and the money that had been collected. Mr. Ehrlich left. The name Arnold topped the list, and he quickly discovered that no amount was listed by my name. Mr. Ehrlich returned with an ashen face.

"Arnold!" he yelled. "Come up here!"

Full of apprehension, I walked to the front.

"Why didn't you bring your money?"

"I have no money. Father is gone. Mum has no salary."

"You tell your mother that the money has to be turned in tomorrow. If it isn't, she will get into serious trouble!"

I was determined to keep Mum out of it. She would not be held responsible for my personal decision.

The next day, Mr. Ehrlich ran into class waving the list in the air. He stood in front of the class and called me out of the row.

"Where is the money?" he shouted.

"I have none," I replied. "My mother doesn't know anything about the youth camp. It is my personal decision. I refuse to go!"

He pulled my ear, dragging me to the front of the class. He was hysterical. I was glad that Ginette was absent. She too was now refusing to heil Hitler, and her father, who wanted her to heil, mistreated her badly. At least she didn't hear the filthy words spouting out of Mr. Ehrlich's mouth—along with his spit.

Circling around me like an animal with its prey, he screamed: "Look at her! At 12 years old, she makes her own decisions. That's the way the Bible Students raise their children!" Miss Lorenz looked down and feigned some activity, embarrassed.

Ehrlich continued circling me. "You be on the train next Tuesday. If you don't report, the police will get you! Here, I am the law, not a child, not a Bible Student, you rebellious creature, you!"

I had decided not to go to the youth camp because of the daily exposure to patriotic ceremonies. I thought it was wiser to say no once instead of facing a daily challenge. I thought about the three Hebrews and the fiery furnace. I felt as if *I* were in the burning furnace. Keeping the whole matter secret from Mum increased the pressure, but I slowly learned to lean on God alone.

"You are really a slowpoke this morning," Mum said, trying to hurry me along. "Girl, if you don't hurry, you'll be late for school!"

Late for school—really, it didn't matter, did it? On my way down, I could feel Mum's eyes following me as she watched me from the balcony. I started walking faster, at least as long as she could see me. After that I slowed to a snail's pace. My class was waiting for the train to take them to the camp. The girls started calling out to me.

"Come with us.... Don't be stupid."

"You fool, we're going to play, and you're going to hell!"

Their words felt like a slap in the face. I ran as far as Rhein Street, out of breath. I daydreamed for a while, passing by the shop windows. There were no children on the street. Then the church clock told me I was 20 minutes late!

I saw Mr. Ehrlich's name on the office door, and I started to shake all over. I knocked softly. No answer. I had to muster the courage to knock once more.

"Come in!"

He was writing and kept me standing there. I thought about the thunderstorm that broke out the first time Mum and I met him. I felt so defenseless, so alone. At last he looked up. His eyes widened. Obviously, he didn't expect to see me. He grabbed me, dragged me into his class of ten-year-olds, and sat me in the first row.

"Now! Up-down, up-down," he ordered the entire class. "Hands on your head! Up-down, up-down," he screamed. He pointed at me with malicious joy on his face and said, "She is to blame!"

I felt so bad that the children had to suffer because of me. After about an hour, Mr. Ehrlich sat down. On his desk, a pile of the students' notebooks waited. As he opened each child's notebook, he called the student to the front. He took the notebook and slapped the student on both cheeks with it. Then he threw the notebook on the floor and, pointing at me, roared, "She is to blame!"

One by one, the 40 children, all with red cheeks, went looking for their notebooks. Some had been damaged by the fall. My insides were all upset; my stomach hurt. I dreaded the prospect of facing 40 angry children.

Then Mr. Ehrlich ordered the class to get up and sing the national anthem, *Deutschland über alles,* and other Nazi songs. During the singing everyone had to salute with arms outstretched. He ran around with his ruler hitting any child whose arm started drooping. He hit me repeatedly, but my arm never went up.

He shouted at me, "You won't leave my class until you write the words of each song ten times!" But the clock ran out. Escaping the morning ordeal, the children ran out as fast as they could. I tried to linger behind, but he sent me out. The children were waiting for me. I was speechless and frightened. Mr. Ehrlich opened the window to watch. At first the children just stared at me. Finally, a voice said, "Keep resisting that swine!" The rest repeated, "Resist, resist!" Upstairs, the window slammed shut.

I couldn't run home fast enough to reveal my secret to Mum. I had so much to tell her. Mother had a gleam in her eyes when she learned about my decision. Making a personal decision, living up to it, and accepting its consequences—these signs reassured her that my love for God was continuing to grow. Many times she had heard my short, simple prayer: "Help me to keep faithful. I'm so little."

Now, Mother also detected my anger. I had developed a deep loathing for my persecutor. "Be polite to Mr. Ehrlich. Don't think of him as an animal, a swine. He may read it in your eyes, and this would make it worse for you. Besides, a Christian doesn't pay back evil for evil. Be attentive and discreet, and don't follow your classmates' rebelliousness. They react because of political influence: French against German. But for us, all humans have the same value. Don't give in!"

I followed Mum's advice, and the rest of my time in Mr. Ehrlich's class went smoothly. I continued to arrive at school at the last minute, avoided contact during playtime, and left as quickly as possible when school ended. I let them all know that I would not be the leader in their rebellion.

I didn't learn much at school, but I applied Mum's wise counsel: "Learn to look through people without seeing their faces." This helped me. Once in a while, I succeeded—Mr. Ehrlich became invisible! Even so, I still didn't enjoy his class. But now my deliverance was near. My class would be back from camping on Monday. What a relief! Just two days more and I could leave Mr. Ehrlich's class.

On Friday, Mr. Ehrlich's class included physical education. Since I wasn't a regular member of the class,

I didn't have a gym outfit. I talked to the gym teacher about it. I was wearing a low-cut, sleeveless shirt, and I felt embarrassed to participate. She ran to Mr. Ehrlich and told him about the problem. He came stamping across the school courtyard.

"Can you imagine," he said scornfully, "a Bible Student stands for moral principles!" Once more I couldn't escape.

"You go under the covered playground where the garbage is piled up," he ordered. "Sort the iron, the papers, the cans, and the bones, and put them in different containers!"

Under the roof of the playground, I leaned against the wall. Next to me stood the empty containers. I knew that the iron scraps would be used to support the war effort. My head throbbed. Mr. Ehrlich came to check on my work.

"Why aren't you working?"

"I have a bad headache."

He believed me, and I was grateful for it. The next day, Saturday, was the last day I would be in his class. When gym class began, I was sent to work.

Mingled together in a huge pile were scraps of iron; stinking maggot-covered bones, some even with rotten meat on them; empty cans; and paper. Next to the pile, empty containers waited to be filled. I stepped away, just upwind, to avoid the horrible stench, which almost made me vomit. Soon I would be free.

I daydreamed—would I get to go to Bergenbach? Grandma could be harsh, but I knew that deep down she had a good heart. Skipping among the rocks, chasing after butterflies, searching for wild strawberries, listening to the running brook—would my dream soon come true? In a few days, school would be over.

Out of nowhere, long, icy fingers gripped my neck, pushing my head down. A terrifying figure stood before me. It was an animal masquerading as a man.

"Don't tell me that you have a headache!" I froze. The bell had rung, but I hadn't heard it. His malicious eyes told me that this time he would get me.

"And why didn't you sort…?"

"I do not work for war," I blurted out.

"You dumb creature, what do paper and bones have to do with war?"

"If I sort paper and bones, the iron will be left over, and they will make ammunition with it," I stammered. "I will not participate in the war effort!"

"I order you," he thundered, "do your assigned work immediately." A shower of spit came flying out of his mouth.

My insides trembled. I took a few steps forward, pushed by his cold, stiff fingers. Half bent over, I kept murmuring, "I can't, I can't."

He let me go, raised his hand, and brought it down with a sharp blow on the back of my neck—just the way Grandpa would stun a rabbit he intended to kill.

When I opened my eyes, at first I saw worms and rotting bones. After a few moments, I realized that I was surrounded by the children. They were terrified by the ordeal. Ehrlich was gone. The children helped me get up out of the stinking trash. Two girls helped me home, one on my right, the other one on my left. It was later than usual, and Mum stood anxiously on our balcony.

Late that afternoon, Mum took me to the doctor. I had started to bleed heavily. Dr. Baumann told me that I was now a little lady. But Mr. Ehrlich's brutality had turned a much-anticipated occasion into a traumatic event. I needed a week's rest. The doctor wrote a medical statement, and Mum dropped it off at school.

I was overjoyed to be able to stay home with Mum. For a whole week, I would get to enjoy her soothing companionship. Nothing could have meant more to me.

❧ ❧ ❧

On Monday afternoon, a policeman came by with an envelope. The notice read, "The doctor's statement is not valid." It said that I had to return to school the next day. Mum had to pay a fine of 300 marks for each day I had missed school, starting from Monday. It would be impossible to gather so much money.

Mum had to report that day to the police. Afterward, she went to Dr. Baumann, but at first he wouldn't let her in. Finally, he explained that the Gestapo had visited him that morning. They had threatened him. If he helped the Bible Students anymore, he would be sent to a concentration camp himself. Dr. Baumann begged Mum to go away.

At the next secret meeting, we were all seated around the garden table. The adults spoke about the latest events. Thousands of Witnesses were imprisoned; many, including Daddy, languished in Dachau. Hundreds had died, among them our beloved "Grandpa" Franz Huber. It is said that an SS officer pointed to the crematory chimney and told Huber, "You fool, this will be your way out." Huber is said to have replied, "It is an honorable one."

❧ ❧ ❧

JUNE 1943

Like so many times before, our Monday afternoon in Adolphe's garden brought us peace. We had to walk home because we couldn't afford tires for our bikes. It took an hour, going downhill across the Rhine Rhône Channel and the Ill River and crossing over the swamp with the blossoming irises.

Those long walks to Bible classes and to the Koehls' garden brought Mum and me closer together, even though the months dragged on and we missed Dad very much.

She was more than my mother—Mum became my true best friend.

She knew how I suffered without Dad, how I had become attached to Marcel, and how it hurt now that he too was gone. She managed to root out my vengeful spirit. With her constant cheerfulness, she helped me to look at things positively. She always kept Dad's example alive. On this particular evening, deep inside, I felt my determination to love and serve God growing into a roaring fire.

Tuesday morning I awoke ready to face any situation, even Mr. Ehrlich. But my blood flow came back and so did my pain. After the ordeal in Mr. Ehrlich's class, I looked forward to seeing my friends, but they avoided me. I sat down at my place. The class felt strange. Everyone ignored me, even the teacher. So I took refuge in my dreams: Bergenbach, liberty, wildlife, running and jumping over rocks and furrows. Soon it would come true—my grandparents needed my help.

CHAPTER 7

Into the Lion's Den

JULY 7, 1943

Another boring day at school was over. Soon I would be with my beloved mother. But just before class ended, Miss Lorenz ordered us to go down to the courtyard. The principal stood there, ready to give a talk to the whole school. The students lined up around a tall pole, the little ones standing in the front. That was good for me—I could easily hide in the back row. It surprised us to see all the boys present too; there were about 500 children in all. Some of the girls wore the Nazi youth group outfit—a dark-blue skirt, white blouse, and black tie; the boys of the Hitler Youth group wore brown shirts. This was a sure sign of a political event, but I felt secure hiding in the back.

All the teachers stood beside their classes. The principal of the boys' school was to the left of Mr. Ehrlich, who called Miss Lorenz over and whispered something to her. As a boy in a brown shirt ceremoniously brought in the flag, Miss Lorenz came over and told me to go to the first row. I suddenly realized that I was to be Mr. Ehrlich's target once again. She pushed me forward.

After she walked away, I discreetly inched backwards to the second row. Again Miss Lorenz was summoned to the center, next to the pole, drawing everyone's attention. She came back, pale and upset.

"Simone, Mr. Ehrlich wants you in front of the first row, all by yourself, in the middle facing the pole."

She was near to tears, but she gently took me by the arm and brought me more than a yard ahead of the first row of girls. All alone, with a thousand eyes scrutinizing me, I felt terror gripping me. "They will insult me, force me, beat me unconscious!" Those terrifying thoughts made me shiver. Mr. Ehrlich gazed at me, obviously delighted to see me unnerved. When the flag was hoisted and the children and teachers stood straight and tall, their arms raised high, I felt completely helpless. I gripped my skirt as tightly as I could.

I feared that I would get carried away by the moment. Something like that had happened to me less than three years before. I hadn't said "Heil Hitler," but caught by surprise amid the reaction of others, I had lifted my arm halfway.

Now, for safety, I held on to my skirt. But that only made my trembling even more visible. While the flag was slowly hoisted up the pole, Mr. Ehrlich stood upright like a conqueror. That victorious, scornful look strengthened my determination, but I couldn't stop shaking.

In my heart, I cried to Jehovah for help: "I do not want to tremble in front of your enemies! Please, O Jehovah! I can't stop shaking!"

The flag reached its summit and waved proudly in the air. Strong voices sang the national hymn in unison. Mr. Ehrlich's eyes were fixed on me. All at once an unfamiliar strength came over me. Inwardly I still trembled, but outwardly my body stopped shaking. I became calm, cold as a block of ice. I looked straight into his eyes, ready to face whatever might come.

My unexpected calm changed Mr. Ehrlich's triumph into anger. In a pompous voice, he started talking about Germany's grandeur, liberty, and prosperity. A Nazi paradise full of people like Ehrlich certainly didn't appeal to me at all.

Mr. Ehrlich's voice got stronger, and his neck turned red. "Who would be a traitor?" Pounding his fist, he screamed, "Let it be known that no one can swim against the German current. The one who doesn't want to bend has to be broken!" Mr. Erhlich paused dramatically.

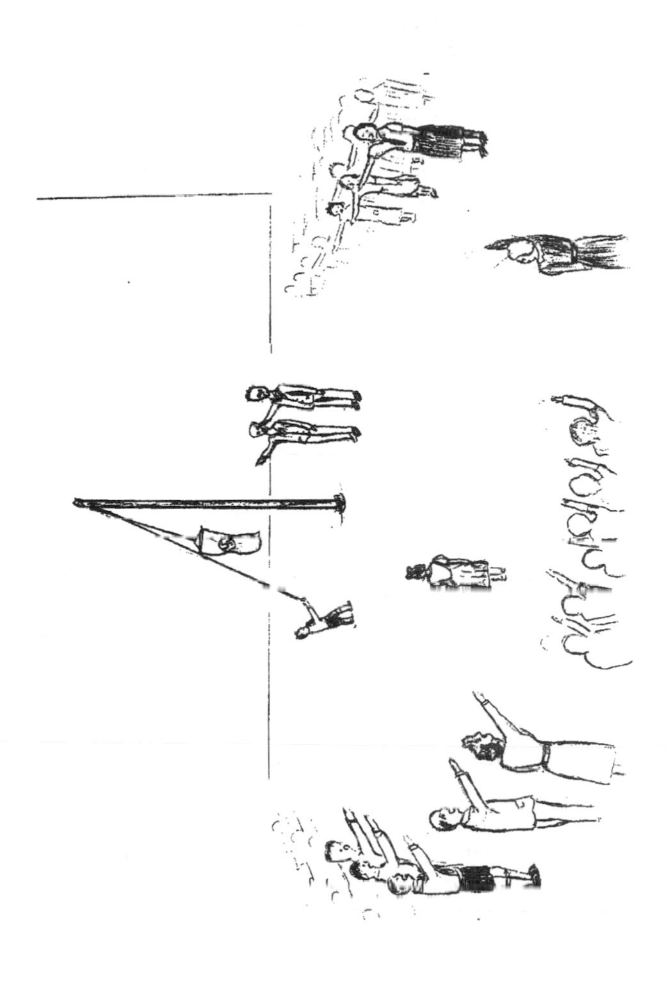

Would this be the moment when everybody would fall on me? Would he beat me again? It didn't matter—I was ready. Ehrlich gave me a vicious look and continued his ranting: "In our school we have such a rebel; she voluntarily makes herself an outcast. Soon both schools will have an example of how the Germans treat vermin. Let us all unitedly stand up against enemies of the state. Defend the *Volksgemeinschaft! Sieg heil! Sieg heil! Sieg heil!*"

Waves of arms went up and down three times, but I wasn't holding my skirt anymore. The flag came down to the sound of *"Deutschland über alles."* I stood as if nailed to the ground, expecting the worst. The children and the teachers departed. All walked away and left me alone. Blanche, Madeleine, and Andrée fled as fast as they could.

I slowly headed home. I had not been beaten physically, but I felt just as crushed as if I had been. My mind was blank; I couldn't think. I was exhausted.

My body felt like lead as I climbed the stairs. Mum was nowhere in sight. In the darkness of the hallway, I saw my bedroom door open. There were clothes laid out on my bed. In front of the hallway mirror on the table sat an envelope. I stared at the paper. Did I read it right? "Simone Arnold must report to the railroad station on Thursday morning at eight o'clock. If there is any delay, she may be subject to police arrest!"

I stood frozen. Then Mum appeared out of nowhere and took me in her arms. Her serene voice reassured me: "My child, you are well past 12. This is the age that high-society children leave home to go to a boarding school for higher learning. We only have this afternoon to get everything ready."

Mum put a manicure kit in my luggage. She said, "You're a little lady now, and you'll have to take care of your nails for yourself." She also packed a sewing box with a double bottom. Tucked inside was a little Bible, a

Catholic version that contained only the New Testament and the Psalms.

I collapsed into bed. Ehrlich's flag ceremony and then the custody order all in one day—the stress had drained my strength, and I fell into an exhausted sleep.

JULY 8, 1943

At eight o'clock the next morning, I stood numb at the railway station between two women from the *Jugendamt.* They didn't want to let Mum come along on my train ride to an unknown fate.

"Why not?" she protested.

Somehow, Mum managed to travel along. A misty rain was falling, and I felt as if it were all a bad dream. Mum took me to the open compartment between the train cars for some air. What a shock to cross the Rhine River into Germany! When we changed trains in Freiburg, the reality finally hit me. A gloomy mountain valley closed in around the train. I started shivering and took refuge under Mum's raincoat. Leaning against her, I felt the beating of her heart. As Mum stroked my hair, she related the Bible story about Joseph, and I closed my eyes to visualize her words. "And Joseph was sold by his brothers and was brought as a slave into Egypt. He was treated like an animal, sold at a public market, seemingly with no hope of freedom. But he found favor with God and man because he was humble and mild-tempered. . . . Remember, Simone, it was Jehovah who granted Joseph to gain favor in the eyes of his superiors. The same can be true for you if you never forsake God's direction."

The rhythmic clickety-clack of the train slowed down, and we had to go inside for a while. But soon my tireless storyteller took me to the open compartment again, facing wind, coal fumes, and misty rain. We talked a lot about Dad on that train ride. I could almost hear his fatherly advice. I was very proud to have such a faithful father. I knew that one day he would help me to finish painting the roses.

The train rolled toward its destination, leaving the Black Forest mountain range behind. Constance was the last stop. The mournful sound of a foghorn told us that a lake must lie somewhere beyond the railroad station.

❧ ❧ ❧

The sky was still gray, the roofs dripping, as we arrived at Schwedenschanze 10, which had a sign—Wessenberg's Reformatory for Girls. I felt numb as we entered the property. Even though they were fellow Alsatians, the two women from the *Jugendamt* were eager to deliver me. They told Mother that she had to stay outside. I heard her answer firmly, "There is no sign forbidding mothers to enter."

As we climbed the steps up to the door, I hardly noticed the park, the blossoming garlands of pink roses, or the Wessenberg monument. A big bell rang, and the door opened. Through blurry eyes I saw an elderly, white-haired lady wearing a long black dress with a white collar. The woman, Fräulein Lederle, told Mum that she had respect for mothers who came along to deliver their children.

Once inside, the two women laid the legal papers on the table, along with the judge's decision. Was this really happening?

Fräulein Lederle said she hadn't received the legal forms and would have to go to court but that everything would be ready for the following morning. The two women protested vigorously when Fräulein Lederle told Mum that she could take me to a hotel for the night. Fräulein Lederle stood erect and said with authority: "This woman will bring her child back. I can see she is a responsible person."

What an unexpected gift! I thanked God for his mercy! It was like a sweet dream. Fräulein Lederle suggested that we could get a cheaper hotel in Meersburg on the other side of the lake. Never before had I seen such a lake, alive with majestic swans, colorful ducks, and crying gulls. A big white boat glided gently along, spewing clouds of smoke from its huge black and red stack. The expanse of calm water seemed to disappear into the sky as the outline of the Meersburg castle appeared. My senses gradually returned.

The hotel was plain but clean, and the hot soup was just what we needed. The air was chilly because of the rain. We went on a long walk uphill next to the castle, gazing at the half-timbered, aging Tudor houses. Passing by the castle, we reached a large vineyard that covered the hill all the way down to the lake. We turned up a dirt road and walked far away from any dwellings.

We realized that we didn't know when we would be together again. We sang a song about the resurrection, and then Mum offered an intense prayer to our God. She really knew how to pray. She asked God to safeguard me, to take me under his wings, and to protect me. She beseeched, "O Jehovah, help my little girl to stay faithful." I never forgot those words. I was determined to be faithful, but I knew that I was so small and the Lion was so big.

As we walked back to the hotel, Mum's arm around my shoulders warmed my heart. I went to bed, and one last time she gave me a big hug and tucked me in. She snuggled up close to me. The sound sleep soothed my tattered nerves.

JULY 9, 1943

The horn of the boat going from Constance to Lindau told us that the time had come. Despite everything, Mother remained calm. Her faith was her strength and shield. The morning sun dried the streets and rooftops. We could see Switzerland across the lake and a snow-covered mountain, the Säntis. The boat glided so fast—only a few minutes more and we would reach the house. And then we would have to say farewell.

Even before Mum had finished ringing the huge bell, the door flew open. Fräulein Lederle seemed to be made of granite—she had completely changed from the day before. She told Mum to leave the luggage at the entrance, and she led us to the reception room. Then she called out for Mathilde. A teenage girl suddenly appeared, grabbed my hand, and dragged me up the stairs. I didn't even get to say good-bye to Mum.

I looked back, but all the doors were closed and my luggage stood in the empty hallway. At that moment, all my strength left me. Then I noticed I was barefoot. Who had taken away my shoes? Silently we climbed the old staircase. I was shown a bed in the corner of a dormitory and a washbasin, the second one in a row of six. The next thing I knew, I stood there in an institutional dress. Who had put it on me? And who had tried without success to braid my short hair?

Downstairs, I entered the classroom. My name was to be Maria, and I was assigned an identification number—No. 1. I had to sit in the last row. Around me I saw only heads with braids. I felt ready to collapse.

The clock sounded for dinner. I had to follow Mathilde closely. Surrounded by silent children, each one standing behind a chair, I realized that I was just like them now—standing in uniform, barefoot and speechless. A voice said the prayer. In front of me sat a bowl filled with a pinkish sauce made of beets and flour. Just looking at it made me feel like vomiting. I was still in shock. I couldn't swallow. Instead, tears filled my eyes, the very first ones I had shed since my arrival.

The afternoon was sewing time. Annemarie, an elderly woman, was in charge of sewing, mending, and ironing. She handed me four pairs of woolen stockings for mending. They had huge holes.

"If they are not correctly mended, with even stitches, they will have to be redone—and a punishment will come with it!" she threatened. "If you are not through by suppertime, you won't get anything to eat." That didn't faze me—I wasn't hungry. My heart was broken. I started crying again. That whole afternoon, my heavy sobbing interrupted the deep silence of the sewing room.

Still, I finished my socks in time. Annemarie checked carefully, trying hard to get her finger through a weak part. She couldn't find fault with my work—she uttered

neither a compliment nor any thanks. She simply told me to go. I started to sob even more.

In the evening, I got acquainted with the special routine, washing our feet in cold water in complete silence. Thereafter, all 36 children, from 6 to 14 years of age, stood in line, the small ones in the front, to listen to the housemother say the evening prayer. The Lord's Prayer ended with an added sentence: "God bless our Führer and our Fatherland!" One after the other, with hands folded behind the back, each child had to step forth and say: "Good night, Fräulein Lederle. Sleep well." Her "good night" was the only time I heard her talk to us that first day.

Mathilde had told me to watch carefully how the girls got dressed and undressed. There was severe punishment for anyone uncovering her body. In bed we had to lie with our arms folded across our chest, with hands placed at the shoulders. Anyone who didn't comply was punished. We were forbidden to talk in the bedroom and washroom. We couldn't talk during school, work, and meals. Spying was used to control everyone, and it was the duty of every child to report violations.

Alone in bed, I shivered from the cold, longing for Mum's arms. The darkness and the silence frightened me.

I hid under the covers, curled up in a ball from the pain in my bowels. I couldn't stop crying.

Thousands of thoughts raced through my mind. The Gestapo had ruined our family life, destroyed my childhood, torn our congregation apart, taken Marcel away to prison, and now left Mum alone. Bergenbach and its meadows, the Koehls' garden with its playgrounds—everything was gone. No more love, warmth, or compassion.

The tears kept coming; a deep resentment crept into my heart. I hadn't been able to say good-bye to Aunt Eugenie or to the Koehls. I didn't even get to hug Mum one last time. Here, no one talked to me except for Mathilde and Annemarie, and they only gave orders. I wasn't allowed to go anywhere, not even to the toilet, without asking loudly for permission. A chaperone would go along to supervise me, even in the toilet.

The sewing box Mum had given me was stowed away on a shelf in a locked closet. Annemarie only opened the closet during our sewing time. My assigned number had to be sewn on all my clothes. My bed with its bran mattress and a little stool nearby, my assigned desk in the last row at school, and the sixth chair at table No. 1 were my only hideaways. I had nothing else, not even privacy.

A flood of tears—tears of self-pity, tears of bitterness, tears of despair—sapped whatever strength I had left. I fell into a deep sleep just one hour before the six o'clock wake-up bell.

In the mornings, we had to make our beds. The deep hole our bodies made in the bran mattresses had to be straightened out and the bed made as flat as a table. Our nightgowns had to be folded in the original pleats with the sleeping cap placed next to it. There would be nothing to eat unless the bed was in perfect order.

I woke up to a total shock. There in the middle of my white sheet was a huge red bloodstain. I ran up to the first matron I saw. It was Fräulein Messinger, the schoolteacher.

Ashamed and trembling, I told her about my soiled sheet. She called Hilde, one of the girls, to tell me what to do. "You'll have to wash your sheet yourself!" she ordered.

A tripod stood in the yard outside with a large empty wooden bucket perched on top of it. I had to fill the bucket with cold water and soak my sheet. Standing barefoot on the cold pavement, I had unbearable cramps. The stain was stubborn, the material rough. I scrubbed off my skin instead of the red spot.

Once more, tears starting flowing. I doubled over in pain. Fräulein Messinger appeared in the doorway wearing a satisfied smirk. She glared at me, making me sob even harder. Then she burst into devilish laughter: "Ha-ha…you cry…well, tell your Jehovah to wash your sheet!"

I glared back at her while drying my last tear with my cold hand. That burly woman dared to make fun of Jehovah God! Not even Mr. Ehrlich had dared to do that. I made up my mind on the spot that I would never give her a chance to mock my God because of my weakness. No more tears for me in this place!

❧ ❧ ❧

It was hard work. The pot was so big! It contained 40 servings of thick soup, and I had to make sure that it didn't burn on the bottom. Standing on my tiptoes on a stool, holding a long wooden spoon with both hands, and wilting from the summer heat and the steam billowing up into my face, I felt like a slave. It wasn't the work itself that bothered me. It was the fact that I was the only one working; all the other children had gone to church.

At the same time the week before, I had been sitting in the classroom reading the Gospels. I had asked Fräulein Lederle if I could take one of the many Bibles I had seen in the school library and read it while Fräulein Messinger went to Mass with the three Catholic orphans who had been raised in an institution. The other girls had been led off to the Protestant church. Fräulein Lederle had granted my request. Alone in the classroom, I had enjoyed reading about Jesus' life. But when Fräulein Messinger found out, she said: "The Bible is not for her. She has to be put on kitchen duty."

The second weekend passed. I gradually realized what my new life would be like. On Sunday mornings I would be standing over huge pots—one for noon, another one for supper, and two for Monday's breakfast. Anna, the middle-aged cook, told me that she would go to church and leave me alone. I felt loaded down and abandoned. No Sunday mornings off for me, and no Bible reading!

We followed a rigid schedule; all of us were bound by endless rules and time constraints. We had to clean house early in the morning before breakfast, which was at eight o'clock. Each child had a specific assignment. I had to clean the toilet, reaching way down inside. Scrubbing for over an hour before we had eaten anything made us all appreciate the bland morning soup made from flour and old bread. If there were boiled flour worms floating in the soup, they had to be eaten too. Nothing could be left in the dish if we wanted to eat at noon. In the evening, we had one dish of soup, a small piece of bread, and a little apple, or half of a bigger one. In summer, we had half a cup of berries.

Monday was laundry day. What a strange sight we were, lined up in our nightgowns and nightcaps, holding our folded underwear. We waited silently to get our next week's set. Fräulein Lederle inspected the used underpants. If they were stained or soiled, we were not allowed fruit for a whole week as punishment.

The washhouse stood at the end of the garden next to the goat stable. About ten of us girls were assigned laundry

duty. Inside the washhouse, three wooden buckets, each sitting on a tripod, were filled with the soaking wash. We had to prewash the laundry before it was boiled in a stone bucket that had been built over a fireplace. We hand washed the 36 undershirts, 36 panties, 36 towels, plus all the kitchen towels and more. Each item was subjected to a rigorous inspection. It was hard work, all done in total silence amid clouds of steam. The only sounds were the matrons' orders and the splashing of wash water.

The afternoon schedule included ironing, mending, sewing, and gardening. Three long wooden tables sat in a line. We each had our assigned place. Hilde sat at the head of the end table. The tall, proud blond played lord

over the rest of us. She was Fräulein Annemarie's favorite. The closet was unlocked, and each girl took her sewing box. I took mine too, but there was no chance to read the little Bible that Mother had hidden inside. It too was in prison.

Fräulein Annemarie would show us how to do a task only once. If we didn't do it right, she would take the clothes and hit us in the face, making our cheeks red. Sometimes she pulled our ears and hair, and if the work wasn't finished before supper, there would be no food. The girl being punished had to stand up when her dish was about to be filled and say in a loud, clear voice: "Thank you, I have no right to eat. I'm being punished." It was sickening to see the empty dish as it passed from hand to hand.

Not a day went by without someone being punished. Fräulein Lederle would put on a leather or rubber apron and take a whip in hand. The girl had to stretch out her hand. The whip cut the air with a terrifying sound, striking the hand with full force and coming to a stop on the apron. If the girl cried, she got a second stroke on the same hand before having to stretch out her other hand. Sometimes, several pairs of strokes were given. Each pair also meant going one evening without supper. Some of the girls would watch the whole process with a sordid satisfaction. At least it was a change in the daily routine.

The only hours less fraught with danger were those we spent at school. Class was held in a small room with six rows of benches for four girls each, with a little library that included several Luther Bibles locked behind a glass window. Again, I had no real lessons in school. Fräulein Messinger only had me write compositions and draw pictures about my childhood. She carefully checked my artwork, probing my thoughts. My German was poor, she said, but I never got a grammar lesson. She showed keen interest in me. Even after school hours, she often asked me to work with her so that she could talk to me. But no matter how nice she tried to be, I couldn't forget that I had Sunday kitchen duty because of her. I couldn't forget the look she had worn when she scoffed at Jehovah! I just couldn't trust her.

Laughing or even smiling had no place among us girls. We only had ten minutes at the morning break for playtime. But there was no friendship, no chatting; even those few minutes of play were under strict control. There was no time to read. We had no books other than the ones at school. There was no drawing or any hobbies. Silence, sleep, and work—hard work—turned us all into zombies. The only amusement was watching the misfortune of others. Most of the children gloated with pleasure if they got the chance to help give out punishment.

I learned that all the children were Germans. But at least here I didn't have to refuse to heil Hitler anymore. Since we were all considered delinquents, we did not have the "privilege" of saying "Heil Hitler" or of becoming a part of the Nazi youth group for girls. First we had to become respectful, honorable members of the *Volksgemeinschaft*. We had to be grateful for the education, which we did not deserve. The degrading talk didn't humiliate me. I was not the only child of Jehovah's Witnesses who was in a reform school. I knew that many others had been taken away. The three Arzt boys and little Jeanette Lauber had been taken from Mulhouse the same week I was sent here to Constance.

When Mum's first letter arrived, I was too numb to realize the great treasure I had. Children around me seldom got news. I had never seen anyone else receive a letter. But then Fräulein Lederle took my letter away to put it in a "safe place" because I had no space of my own for it. Only then did I react. This letter was mine. It had words meant only for me. It had been in Mum's hands; it was part of her, and now I was denied the right to keep it, to cherish it. I felt miserable.

Under my bedcover, I tried to remember Mum's words—and they returned to me, soothing my wounded heart. I suddenly realized that I had a precious, secret possession. Hadn't Dad once told me that I could keep a private library in my memory? No one could take these memories away from me. My dear parents had put so many good things into my heart. I could draw on my own treasures.

I learned not to trust blindly or to hope for anything from anyone in that home. I became more withdrawn. However, I drew even closer to God. I had to be shrewd. I decided to talk or write only about Bergenbach, never about Mulhouse. In my prayers I begged Jehovah to help me speak French in my dreams and never German or Alsatian. I didn't want to turn in names of other Jehovah's Witnesses by talking in my sleep. I felt as if I was in an enemy land, ignored by Fräulein Lederle, taunted by Fräulein Messinger, and targeted by Fräulein Annemarie.

Fräulein Messinger kept asking me to be her helper. She assigned me to water the tomato plants in the late evenings; that meant extra hours. I had to push a wheelbarrow with several loads of water, 40 liters each, over the rough gravel. My bare feet weren't used to the stones. It was backbreaking work, but I felt proud that I was strong

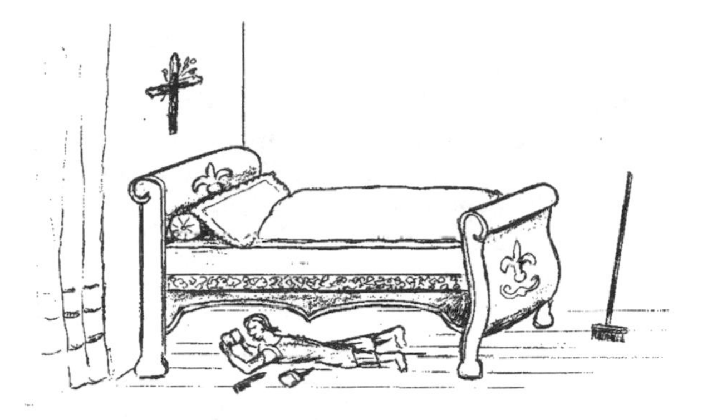

enough to do it, even though I was only 13. I was the only girl who had to do extra duty.

Then I received the intimidating order to clean Fräulein Messinger's bedroom. She expected me to be a reliable housekeeper. This would also mean extra work. I had to continue my morning chores, including the cleaning of the toilets. Her room had to be done right after lunch.

Cleaning day after day under Fräulein Messinger's bed, I got an idea: I would hide my little Bible in the springs. At first I hesitated out of fear. It meant I had to empty my sewing box completely in order to take the Bible out. Fräulein Annemarie sat at the end of my table; the girls with spying eyes sat all around me, making the whole undertaking even more hazardous. Once I freed it from its prison, I had to sneak the little Bible into my only pocket, the one in my slip. It would have to stay there until the following day, hitting my leg with a swishing noise with every step I took. It was dangerous, but I succeeded.

My little book ended up in the springs in the middle of Fräulein Messinger's bed. I worried that the following morning when she got up out of bed and released the springs, the Bible would fall on the floor. But what a delight it was to read the Gospels! When Fräulein Messinger came to check on my work, inspecting for dust, I had plenty of time to put the book back way up in the springs.

Regular Bible reading eased my inner pain. I regained confidence in my hopes for the future. Far away I was building and planning life in a peaceful paradise world; my sewing needle stopped working. "Maria, you lazybones, wake up!" hollered Fräulein Annemarie. I had to speed up if I wanted to have food.

Another extra duty, even more severe, was loaded on me. I had to take care of Anna, a bratty five-year-old girl. A new arrival, she was the daughter of a prostitute and was cunning and unscrupulous. Should Anna steal or destroy anything, I was to be held responsible! I resented it deeply and asked Fräulein Messinger why I had to be Anna's chaperone. No other girl had such a heavy load! She said that Anna was too small to conform to the house schedule and that I was to have the "privilege" of raising her! She could get up later than the other girls could, and I had to wash and dress her, fix her hair, make her bed, and mend all her clothes. Worse yet, I had to get up twice every night to take her to the toilet. If she wet the bed, I would have to wash her sheet.

FIRST WEEK OF AUGUST, 1943

At the afternoon lineup for work assignments, I received a special job for the day. I was to go by myself to the front of the house and pick the red currants from the bushes alongside the beautiful park. I was surprised. Children were never allowed to go anywhere alone—not even to the toilet. "Just enough work for one," Fräulein Lederle said. The children's jealousy showed in their eyes.

Alone at the edge of the park, I gathered part of our evening meal, a little cup of sour berries that would accompany a thin slice of dark dry bread after the potato soup. While working, I kept looking at the majestic fir tree. Its scent made me dream of Bergenbach. I even heard my name being called. The call persisted—at first a woman's voice and then a man's. I looked around. In the property's hedgerow behind a dead privet bush, I saw two people waving at me. I could hardly believe my eyes. I felt like shouting, and I nearly jumped through the dried-up privet hedge. It was Adolphe and Maria Koehl! They had come in the morning, but Fräulein Lederle had told them that I could not receive any visitors. Before taking the train home, they came by once more to have a last look at the home and the garden, peeking through the leafless bush as if it were a window.

Our conversation was very short and mostly one-sided. Weeks without conversation had affected me. I spoke in short sentences. But I managed to tell them that so far I hadn't been punished and that I was able to read my Bible every day. I did not say a word about my difficult work assignments. And I said nothing about my disturbed nights taking care of Anna. Why should I make them worry?

The news from home brought me a ray of sunshine. Dad continued to enjoy his "vitamins." Grandma was exhausted and had accepted Mum's offer to stay with her in Bergenbach. At least Mum would not be alone. But there was bad news about Marcel Sutter—he expected to receive the death sentence.

❧ ❧ ❧

Nothing had changed at the reformatory. As usual, the soup was bland, the berries sour. But my heart ached anew. The exuberant joy of seeing the Koehls turned into a terrible feeling of loneliness. It took days to climb out of my self-pity, to be able to ponder Adolphe's words: "Never forget," he said, "no one can hinder God's spirit; it cannot be put in prison. As long as we are under God's guidance and do not abandon him, we will have power to endure." Slowly I became myself again.

Early every morning, I had to open the window but was not allowed to linger there to enjoy the view. After getting dressed and making the bed, I had to close it again. My bed was just under the window. A short glance at the park revived my visions of a paradise earth. From my bed, I could see some stars. From there, I could make plans and go on trips in my imagination.

Fräulein Lederle let me read a long letter from Mum. I could hear the warmth in her words. That second letter brought Mum right to me. In it she encouraged me to be a good example for my peers. She also told me never to be unfair in my dealings with the other girls. Our family knew what injustice meant; we had suffered terribly because of it. Mum told me to do my best to learn housework, gardening, and manual labor, for these skills would serve me well in the future. "Face everything with courage, and be strong," she wrote. She assured me that we still had to face hardships, but for God's honor we were ready for them.

If only Mum knew how difficult it was in this place! How could I be happy when I had to get out of bed while everyone else was sleeping? Cooking Sunday mornings while everyone went off to church—it was so unfair.

Now I had the job of supervising potato duty. Every evening at five o'clock, six girls peeled potatoes for an hour. If a girl tried to hurry and cut thick peelings, she had to be turned in. Fräulein Lederle or Fräulein Messinger would administer the punishment—no evening soup! They also examined the peelings checked by the supervisor,

who could also be punished. Almost every day one or two children went without soup. How could I denounce other girls just to avoid getting punished myself? I solved the dilemma by warning the girls when the peelings were too thick. Every evening was stressful, but none of us were punished.

The noon meal was the darkest moment of the day. I missed my parents even more during the total silence. The only sounds came from children who didn't know how to eat properly. My throat tightened when I tried to eat the colorless, bland food. How could I eat when I fought to hold back the tears that wanted to roll down my cheeks?

SEPTEMBER 1943

A letter from Aunt Eugenie brought me shocking news. My dear mother had been arrested and taken to the camp in Schirmeck. She wouldn't be able to write to me anymore. I had to face the terrible news all alone. I could only turn to God.

I realized that Mother's second letter would be the last one I could expect. I knew her letter almost by heart, and I fed on its wonderful uplifting words. She had written that she prayed for me, and she urged me to be faithful, a firm fighter for God's Kingdom and his name. I felt comforted to know that she prayed for me. I needed her prayers; mine were still short.

❧ ❧ ❧

Anna, my charge, hated me because I had to get her up during the night. She soon found a way to get even. As soon as she saw me coming into her dormitory, she stood up on her bed and urinated. In my rage, I decided to punish her myself. As usual, I got the tripod and the bucket with cold water. Then I caught Anna, squeezed her between the bucket and me, and forced her hands into the

cold water. She screamed, struggling to free herself from my grip. I didn't give in. I was furious. Fräulein Lederle heard her grating voice. So Anna received severe punishment even though I didn't tell on her.

Not only did she keep wetting her bed in spite of her being my prisoner during the wash but she would soil the sheets of her neighbors' beds. She got severe punishment again, easing the problem for a short time.

My neighbor in the next bed, Sofie, was a blond, curly-haired girl with pink cheeks. She used to smile timidly at me. She was also my tablemate, being at the head of table No. 2, while I sat at the end of table No. 1. My bed was alongside the wall, separated from her bed by a small stool. My personal stool was at the foot of my bed; the next three beds were lined up against the wall, perpendicular to mine. Hilde slept in the first one, Hannelore in the next.

One evening Sofie put her pillow on her stool, leaned toward me, and whispered, "Why are you here? You are so different from all of us. Why don't you come to the Protestant church with us instead of having cooking duty?

Why do you get mail? How come Fräulein Messinger always calls you?" I used the occasion to talk with her about the Gospels. My little corner was like a den, giving a little relief from the day's pressure. Now it was even a place to share my faith.

The following evening under our pillows, I talked to her about the hope for a peaceful future. Sofie interrupted me: "We've been betrayed. I just saw someone come out from under your bed and go downstairs." Soon the call came: "Sofie, Maria, down!" Fräulein Lederle's harsh voice boomed like a thunderstorm. We passed Hilde on the stairs. She looked triumphant. Sofie was all upset, but I was confident. Granted, it was forbidden to talk. But this was not just idle talk or gossip. We had discussed a holy subject.

Next to the high tile stove at the entrance of the office, Fräulein Lederle waited for us. She told us to repeat the rules. Of course, both of us knew that it was strictly forbidden to talk. First Sofie had to confess, and she gave a truthful account. It was a pity to see her shaking all over.

Then came my turn. "What is your version?" Fräulein Lederle demanded.

"The same," I replied. I felt confident. "We talked about Jesus giving his life to bring back the Paradise on earth that Adam lost. Death and sickness will be gone, and the dead will be resurrected. I told Sofie that we can have this future if we closely follow Jesus." All the time I had looked straight at Fräulein Lederle.

Fräulein Lederle stepped behind the tile stove to get her heavy apron and reached for the whip. Sofie had to go first, and I had to watch the whipping. She stepped forward. Fräulein Lederle placed her on her right, facing me. Sofie extended her right hand for the first stroke. The stick made a whistling sound as it came down on Sofie's little fingers and stopped on the apron. Fräulein Lederle used all her strength. Poor Sofie, standing there in her nightgown, closed her eyes and gritted her teeth from the pain. She withdrew her trembling hand and reached out the other one.

After that pair, Fräulein Lederle told her to put out her right hand again. I was outraged! How could she get two pairs? The most punishment I had ever seen was two pairs, four strokes, which meant two evenings without supper. How could this church-going person give out this kind of punishment just because we had broken the rules to talk about God? Sofie had stepped back waving her hands. I assumed it was my turn.

But Fräulein Lederle called Sofie back and administered a third set. I glared at the woman. She stood still, waiting until the cramp in Sofie's hand subsided and she could open it again. Then, as Fräulein Lederle slowly raised the stick for a fourth set, she ordered, "Look at me, both of you." Sofie bit her lip to keep from crying. If she had made a sound, Fräulein Lederle would begin all over again. A cold shiver came over me, and I felt the beginnings of cystitis.

A fifth pair followed, making Sofie writhe in pain. With a heartless voice, Fräulein Lederle said: "If you pull away, I'll have to start all over from the beginning." I felt all my blood rush into my head.

With merciless accuracy, Fräulein Lederle lifted her arm again and administered the sixth pair. Sofie's blond, curly hair stuck to her forehead; even her nightcap was soaked. Again came the necessary pause before she was ordered to present the now unrecognizable hand. Sofie's terrified eyes begged for mercy. She struggled to stretch out her arm. But Fräulein Lederle was insensitive to the sight of Sofie's suffering, and the seventh pair of strokes fell with the same pitiless and unsparing force. Sofie was at last sent to bed, holding her horribly swollen hands high up, trembling all over. A week without supper would follow.

It was terrible to watch that inhuman punishment machine in action. Now it was my turn. With clenched teeth, I presented my hand, waiting for her iron "justice." But I also looked at Fräulein Lederle's eyes. I was deter mined to face the beating courageously because I was being punished for talking about God.

Suddenly the stick went back to its place on top of the tile stove. Fräulein Lederle said: "Your religion makes you lose all sense of responsibility. You forget the rules and regulations. I can see that you are obedient in everything else, but your religion is your downfall. Know that if this happens again, I'll make up the seven strokes from tonight, and you'll get 14 pairs!"

I had a hard time walking upstairs. My cystitis burned, my stomach ached, and I had a fever. I felt so embarrassed that I had escaped punishment. I tried to delay on the stairs because I felt that it was so unfair for me to come back so quickly. This would hurt Sofie even more. I cried for her—for her humiliation, for her pains, but also because I felt disgusted. Sofie was sobbing uncontrollably. But Hilde was watching us. We couldn't even console each other; otherwise the ordeal would start all over again. Totally exhausted, I fell into a deep sleep.

The following morning Sofie had a hard time making her bed with her swollen hands. I was ashamed that mine were normal, but I wasn't allowed to help her.

Sofie sat at the head table. She passed down the dishes of her six table companions. I heard her say, with a calm, strong voice, "Thank you, I have no right to eat because I'm being punished." Sofie, with her injured hands, and Thila carried the soup pot to our table, followed by Fräulein Lederle. At our table, the dishes were passed up to the pot. My dish went from hand to hand, the second to the last to be presented. Spontaneously, I jumped to my feet and said: "Thank you, I have no right to eat. I'm being punished." Fräulein Lederle peered at me, totally surprised. My empty dish was already halfway back to me when she called it back and filled it with soup. She also ordered Sofie's dish to be filled and passed to her. "I do not want to hear anything more about the matter."

The following day, Sofie passed by and murmured: "You weren't being punished, I could see that. But what

you did and how it turned out—it's a miracle. Believe me, I've already been here seven years, and such a thing has never happened before!" But I just put my finger to my lips and walked past her quickly without answering.

Fräulein Messinger led us six older girls to different work assignments. Sometimes we did men's work. She was a strong woman and would give us girls a hand, but one day it was too much even for her. Fräulein Messinger lay in bed, suffering with paralyzing sciatica. She called me in. She must have been lonely in her room.

"Stay with me, and let's have a chat." She had me sit next to her bed.

"Come nearer," she said with a warm smile. Bewildered, I inched closer. Again she asked about Alsace and my childhood. I had many stories to tell.

After a while she remarked, "Maria, you never talk about Mulhouse." So, it hadn't escaped her notice!

"I'm a country girl. I love mountain life, wild flowers, and my grandparents' farm. There's nothing special about city life."

"Why?" she asked. "You weren't happy with your parents?"

"Oh, yes, I was! I loved being with Mum and Dad, running through fields and forests, searching for mushrooms. We picked blueberries and raspberries. They were delicious!"

She added, "You had only your parents for company?"

"I also had wonderful times with Angele, my cousin, and with Uncle Germain and Grandpa!"

"But you also know the Arzt boys?" she continued. How did she know them? The three Arzt boys had been sent to Nazi reform schools in Germany, but their father, whom I had never met, was still at liberty. I couldn't say yes and expose him, nor could I say no. Then I had an idea.

"My *Arzt* was named Baumann." (In German, *Arzt* means "doctor.")

Fräulein Messinger continued her gentle probing. "But you had other friends in the city, didn't you?"

"Yes, I went to school with Andrée, Blanche, and Madeleine. We were very close." I went back to Bergenbach, bubbling over with stories about Grandma.

After a few minutes, she interrupted me abruptly, "But you must know Graf!"

She knew everything! Marcel Graf was a member of our little congregation and the link in the underground activity. So far he had not been arrested. I was caught in another dilemma. Then it occurred to me that *"Graf"* in German means "count," or "nobleman."

"We didn't know any counts. We are just plain people. Dad worked in the factory. We're not from the upper class." Fräulein Messinger blushed. It was a good thing for me she couldn't move; she sent me away for sewing time.

A thousand questions raced through my mind. Why did she ask me about my parents and Mulhouse? Why all those questions about our friends? How did she know Marcel Graf? Who else but the Gestapo would be looking for him? What would she have done if I had given her information? How sneaky!

Adolphe Koehl had always told us to be shrewd. Still, my answers surprised me. I gave thanks to God for the peace of mind I felt.

❧ ❧ ❧

Sunday afternoon we all had to do embroidery under Fräulein Annemarie's supervision. Fräulein Messinger came in holding a pair of silk stockings. "Who would like to reinforce the heels and the sole?" A long silence followed.

I heard mother's counsel, "As a Christian, you have to be a good example, always willing to work." I volunteered.

It wasn't easy. The stitches were so close together. It took a long time. My nerves were frazzled. I regretted having volunteered. But I had no other way to get out of this sticky situation than to do the work and to do it fast and well. Otherwise, I would not get my dish of soup, a little piece of bread, and a tiny pear.

Fräulein Messinger closely checked my weaving. "You really deserve a reward," she declared. During the evening meal, she came over with a huge red apple. "Maria, here is your reward. I'll put it up here because you have already had your supper. I'll give it to you later." I expected my apple on Monday afternoon, but it seemed that Fräulein Messinger had forgotten all about it.

Days passed while my apple sat there. Finally, Fräulein Messinger said, "Instead of having your milk, you can eat your apple today." I had to wait until she had ladled out the goat milk for everyone. Then with gloating eyes, she handed me my "reward." But it was a heartless trick—the apple was completely rotten inside.

"Let that be a lesson," she said with a smirk. "Not everything that looks shiny is good."

She walked away, leaving me to eat my thin, dry piece of bread, fighting my inner urge to rebel.

❧ ❧ ❧

NOVEMBER 1943

Early one morning, I overheard Fräulein Messinger say eagerly to Fräulein Lederle: "I'll take her. I want to be present." One of the outfits Mum had sewn—along with nice shoes and new stockings—was waiting for me. We walked down a wonderful avenue lined with rows of tall trees. Fräulein Messinger said, "Make a wise choice." But I had already made my choice. I had made it long ago when

I had told my parents that I wanted to be baptized, and they had agreed. I was a Witness for Jehovah and was on my way to a bright future.

We crossed the avenue ending at the shore of the Rhine River. Halfway down the street, we turned to a building; *Bezirksamt* (District Court) was written in big letters. Going upstairs Fräulein Messinger said again: "Be wise. The choice is in your hands; you make your destiny!"

A handsome, elderly judge waited for me at an elegantly carved and highly polished desk. He flattered me in a fatherly tone. He was happy to read to me all the reports from Fräulein Lederle. They were all positive: I was conscientious, courageous, honest, and willing to volunteer for any kind of work. My parents would be pleased. The judge explained that the court in Mulhouse had made the decision to take me away from the erroneous teaching of the Bible Students because I was being mentally corrupted. The life in the Wessenberg home had given me the opportunity to develop all those positive qualities! By this schooling, I could find my place in the *Volksgemeinschaft* and have a brilliant future.

The judge continued with his flattery. He said I was smart enough to understand that resisting legal authorities has no future. "One just cannot swim against the stream." It was always the same statement by the Lion.

"See where your father and mother have ended up!" he said. "It was their choice, and by making it they sacrificed your future." He blamed my parents for my being sent to Constance. They had blinded me, he claimed, and the National Socialist State had saved me. How this judge had been misled! No child could have been happier or have better parents than I had.

The judge persisted: "Now months of freedom from their control have allowed you to think, so that you can make your personal choice today."

Didn't he know that I had always made my own decisions?

"But in order that your choice will be an informed one," he continued, "I'll read the outcome of a stubborn decision." I had heard it before: At age 14, the juvenile leaves the home to become a maid or to go to prison, or even to a concentration camp. "Whoever doesn't bend, will break," he said, a favorite Nazi proverb. "A wrong choice will lead you to where your parents are."

I refused to budge. The judge and Fräulein Messinger looked at each other, both shaking their heads. Fräulein Messinger made excuses for herself, saying that she had done all she could. The judge started all over again, speaking with conviction about the great honor it would be to become an active and productive member of the master race.

"You have two documents—you can sign this one and be free today, or you can sign that one stating your decision to stay a Bible Student." I picked up the paper

stating that I would stay a Bible Student and signed it in front of the judge.

"She is the brood of her parents, shrewd and bold!" the old judge hollered, losing his temper. "She is definitely corrupted!" His eyeballs popped out against his now white complexion, and he suddenly began spewing filthy speech at me.

That evening, in my cold bed back at the home, a warm feeling of well-being made my heart sing. That feeling must be what Dad had written about. In one of his letters, Dad had explained that we have a judge inside us—our heart. The joy we feel is the best guarantee that we have done what is good, and the joy becomes the anchor of our hope, keeping our life's boat stable through the stormy sea. Reflecting on Dad's letter, I knew that I had made the right choice that morning.

Much later I learned that shortly after this, my father was called in to the commandant's office at Dachau and shown the paper I had signed. They held him responsible for my decision.

❧ ❧ ❧

The leaves had all fallen off the trees. Out of the window, only yards away across the border fence, I could see the land of freedom, Switzerland. I caught a glimpse of it while mending a basket with no bottom. But I was on my way to prison or to a camp, the judge had said. Still, I felt free. I was only 13. There was some time to go yet, and maybe the war would end!

Fräulein Lederle called me into her office. I tried hard to forget the ferocious look she had worn that night when she had beaten Sofie. I was nervous; it was the first time since then that I had to face her. The room had a table, a desk, a typewriter stand, and a tile stove. There were lots of file cabinets and a little buffet to clean. Mathilde had been

Chrimhilde Lederle, overseer of the Wessenberg Institution for Juvenile Education

Wessenberg Institution for Juvenile Education

cleaning the place, but she was caught reading papers. She had been severely punished and had lost her job.

It was considered the most honorable housework. But I felt sad about losing my assignment in Fräulein Messinger's room. I lost my hiding place—Fräulein Messinger's bedsprings—and I couldn't do my Bible reading anymore. I had to sneak into her room to get my little Bible. My stool had a little drawer for girl's sanitary items. I stashed the Bible there. But a few days later, for the first time, Fräulein Lederle searched the dormitory and found it. It was taken away from me without punishment.

I felt completely abandoned. Now I had nothing left except my memories and the Bible stories Mum had told me. My work too was more dangerous. Files were left open on the desk. I had to move them to clean the table. I closed my eyes when handling them. I was afraid that a matron might accuse me of reading the secret reports.

Now my work started in the morning. I had to open the windows and clean the fireplace in the tile stove then start another fire. The floor had to be buffed every day, and I had to set the table for breakfast. I also had to move ten pots of primroses and cyclamen. They were perched on the sill between the double windows and had to be removed and put back again. In my future house, I thought, I would have plants like these adorning all my windows. Now that I had learned how to take care of them, they became a part of my dream.

I was on my knees, vigorously buffing the floor; it had to shine like a mirror. Unexpectedly, the door swung open. Fräulein Messinger stood motionless at the threshold, tall and proud. She wore the same look she had the first time she had scoffed at me and taunted Jehovah. She looked down at me with disdain and crossed her arms. What was this all about? She never came down so early.

As I continued to work, she called my name. I looked up at her. She smirked.

"Maria, I have special news for you," she proclaimed with satisfaction. I stood up and faced her.

"Your mother's boyfriend, Marcel, has been beheaded." She repeated with emphasis, "Yes, your mother's lover has had his head cut off with an ax!" She continued staring at me for a while, scrutinizing the impact of the news on my heart. Finally, she turned away and left me.

What did she see in my face? My feelings were mixed. My heart pounded. Marcel, my brother, had won the victory. I felt proud. Marcel, my friend and teacher, was my model. He had stayed faithful until death. He had proved that one can stay loyal under test. He had God's approval, and his resurrection was assured. I didn't even cry. I admired him because he had refused to have a share in Hitler's war machine. My love for him grew.

CHAPTER 8

Help Came Ever So Often

A white coating had turned the park into a fairyland, but now the snow had melted. A short glimpse in the morning was all I had seen of the winter. I missed the snowball fights with Dad, the buggy rides in the moonlight, and the sharp impressions in the fresh snow. The days dragged on with monotonous labor and schoolwork. Even the smaller ones didn't get to taste winter play and its joys. Snow had made me homesick, and I was relieved to see it go away.

The classroom calendar told me that the first full moon of spring had arrived. Many times Dad had shown me how to calculate Nisan 14, the date of the Passover as well as the Memorial of Jesus' death. After the collective evening prayer, I stayed behind, letting all the girls say good night. I asked Fräulein Lederle for permission to go to the schoolroom and read the Bible because it was Easter time. She agreed, but as soon as I finished, I had to come to the office and say good night.

I spent a delightful evening reading the Exodus story and the Gospel accounts about Jesus' death. By then, night had come and the moon shone brightly. I put the huge Lutheran Bible back in the school library and went to say good night. I heard Fräulein Messinger ask angrily, "What is she still doing up?"

The following morning Fräulein Messinger was enraged, pacing back and forth and shouting: "You sneaky lying rebel! You misled us and brought a Jewish celebration into the house!" Never would that happen again, she threatened. She continued yelling, but I didn't care. I knew I had done the right thing.

A matron called me. I had a surprise visitor. Seated at the lace-covered table where Mum had sat was Aunt Eugenie! We had one hour together in the parlor, with Fräulein Messinger in between us. Aunt Eugenie bore news from Bergenbach, a letter from my mother, a package for me, and four gift parcels for the matrons.

That hour lifted my spirits. But after she left, my mood changed. Aunt's visit opened my wounds. I realized just how much of my life the Nazi regime had destroyed. I even wished she had never come! For days after her visit, I walked around downhearted. The matrons had refused to give me my gift package.

Slowly, though, my heart began to heal. I had just recovered from Aunt's first visit when she wrote that she would soon come again. I was apprehensive.

Again Aunt brought a gift package for me and presented four little gift parcels to the matrons. To my surprise, Fräulein Messinger said that I could go with Aunt to a restaurant just a few minutes away for lunch. Because of wartime shortages, they only served potato salad and a hot sausage. Aunt said that the sausage contained more flour than meat. But I thought it tasted wonderful.

Aunt made me eat plenty of cookies while she told me the news. There was no word from Dad and only a few lines from Mum, but Aunt couldn't show me the letter. It bore the concentration camp regulations in big print, and there were too many eyes in the restaurant.

When it was time to return, the blues descended upon me again. Walking slowly toward the Wessenberg home, I felt the same anxiety that had struck me nine months earlier when Mum had brought me here. Aunt tried to encourage me, but I couldn't talk. I had to fight to hold back my tears. My aunt would go back to the Koehls and visit Bergenbach, and I had to stay in this pitiless home. I felt like running away from this cold house with its silent children and harsh routine.

Aunt rang the bell. Fräulein Lederle opened the squealing door, called Aunt in, and quickly sent me away to undress. Did I say good-bye to Aunt? Would the matrons confiscate my gift parcel again? I didn't care. Once again Aunt had opened the wounds that I had tried to keep hidden. Hard work helped me to overcome my hollowness.

❧ ❧ ❧

SPRING 1944

It was a sunny spring Sunday morning. Fräulein Messinger was very excited. I had never seen her with such a radiant face, admiring her third gift parcel from Aunt Eugenie. Was this the reason she granted me a full day with Aunt? I had to get ready quickly. We had to hurry if we wanted to catch the next boat.

I stayed quiet next to Aunt as we waited to board the boat. We mingled with the passengers, mostly women, children, and some elderly men loaded down with luggage. There were no tourists anymore, only local residents trying to reach the other shore.

The surroundings hadn't changed. The smell of the lake, which I hadn't seen for almost a year, brought me back to the last day Mum and I had spent together. On the deck, Aunt looked like Mum; they were so much alike. We crossed the lake, gliding over the calm waters, heading for Meersburg.

I bubbled with excitement as we neared the harbor. How delightful to take Aunt to the places I had shared with Mum during our last hours together! As we climbed up in the shadow of the castle, we passed the little hotel. I could still feel Mum's good-night kiss. We passed the city gate and climbed up to the vineyard.

"Aunt, Mum and I sat here where no one could see us. I'm sure this is the place where we knelt and said a prayer." Aunt laid out her coat, opened her bag, and spread out a picnic. But before eating, we would do some reading. It was so pleasant and encouraging to read my parents' faith-strengthening letters together. Aunt had brought another treat: a typewritten copy of *The Watchtower* in German. At noon, the hot sun made us move under a tree to eat lunch, complete with Aunt's delicious cookies and jam and a wonderful chocolate drink.

I had not been able to do any Bible reading for many weeks. I had only been able to relive the Bible stories Mum had taught me. But now I had a fresh supply—the reading of *Watchtower* articles nourished my heart.

The shadows became long and the air cool; we started down the hill. Suddenly, I realized that I might be asked to write an essay about my outing, and I didn't have enough material that I could write about. Normally, I would write eight or ten pages along with drawings. If I did less, they might ask questions.

"Let's have a quick look at the castle," Aunt suggested. But it was too late, and the door was closed. The only thing handy was a set of ten postcards that were folded like an accordion. I got one last look at Meersburg in the golden evening sun as our boat left white foam on the now dark-green water. I had about a half hour to study the ten postcards, which Aunt would take back with her to Mulhouse. I found many things to write about—just in case.

Aunt promised to come back with another *Watchtower.* This time, the prospect of another visit put my heart at ease. The Koehls would pay for her trip because Aunt did not have much money. I felt calm as I watched her go. The big door closed on me again—but, I thought, only for a short time. The trip to Meersburg had strengthened my determination. Fräulein Messinger had allowed me the happiest day since I had come to Wessenberg. What was her motive?

Meersburg Castle

The next morning, Fräulein Messinger said: "Maria, you went for an outing yesterday. Prepare an essay." It ended up as a 12-page composition about the lake, the animal life, Aunt's cookies, and a detailed description of the castle.

Spring-cleaning meant hard work and long days for us six oldest ones. We had to wash all the sheets that we had used for the whole winter. Washing those heavy linens by hand wasn't easy. It took a whole week. It was especially difficult to wring them out. Our hands were small, and even though we used all our strength, we hardly managed to squeeze the water out. The inspector examined each sheet before we put it on the line to dry. At the end of the day, it felt so good to sleep in clean, white beds and to have fresh, clean caps to replace the dingy gray ones.

It was also the time for our annual hair wash. We undid the braids of the younger ones and washed their stiff, greasy hair. It was like a metamorphosis. Many of

them had blond hair that waved in the warm sun like shiny yellow silk. But it had to be braided again. Some braids were long enough to wrap around the head like a crown. Shorter braids simply hung down on both sides. My thin little braids were not blond, and my eyes were not blue. Fräulein Messinger said that I was lower than the Germans on the ladder of evolution. I was envious, not of the other girls' hair color, but of the amount—my hair looked like a rat's tail.

The garden was also waiting to be dug and planted. That made a heavy workload for only six girls to carry, in addition to doing our daily morning assignments and schoolwork. I didn't mind working hard. I had got used to it on Grandma's farm. And besides, it made the time go fast. But I was happy to rest my sore muscles in a clean bed and escape to my dreamland.

I also enjoyed learning how to plan and cook fancy meals. This meant that in a few months, I would be ready to be a maid. I had been cooking ever since my second Sunday in the home, but now I had to plan the menu. Every Sunday, I cooked the matrons' meals. These were very sophisticated—two kinds of meat and always a torte, using plenty of butter, eggs, sugar, and milk.

Among my routine duties was the four o'clock tea for the four teachers. Each had her own porcelain tea set—expensive, fine antiques with beautiful rose designs and gold circles. A hand-embroidered lace tablecloth, the plate, and the silver spoon, along with tea, coffee, and sweets, made up a fine table setting.

Fräulein Anna, the cook, taught me well. She seemed to feel guilty that I had to cook fancy meals for the matrons all by myself, but she would explain: "In order to teach you properly, we have to do the type of cooking a family demands from their maid."

She was a fast worker. She never shouted or punished, but neither did she ever share a nice word or a compliment, even though I made it possible for her to have Sundays off to attend church. All she had to do was check the broiling meat. She kept to herself in the huge kitchen. I never saw her talk to anyone. I was often called to work with her during the week.

The only Sundays that I did not have kitchen duty were when Aunt visited, usually every fifth Sunday. On those days I would feel like a young lady, dressed in one of the outfits Mother had made for me. I hadn't grown one inch since I was taken away from home, so I could still wear those dresses.

Fräulein Messinger reached a surprising conclusion about Aunt's visits and said to her: "Maria's description about her outing with you in Meersburg proved how much she is learning to love German culture, German history, and German art. Take her to Heiligenberg today."

Late blossoming apple trees surrounded the impressive Heiligenberg castle, and a nice set of postcards filled in the details. The following visit to Uberlingen ended with an interesting tour of an ancient settlement of wooden houses built on stilts over the water. There was much to write about. But in the shade of some medieval building or fruit plantation, we read the Bible and studied the mimeographed pages of *Watchtower* articles that had been translated by Marcel Graf and Adolphe Koehl. Ah, that was my precious secret! Fräulein Messinger corrected my essays, but she never discovered the true reason for my high spirits following those outings.

Fräulein Lederle decided to include me as one of the three girls who were responsible for delivering the bill payments. We were all over 13 years old. Every week, we went out to pay the butchers, bakers, and grocers. We had a set time, sometimes only a few minutes, to perform our duty. So we had to walk fast or even run to get it done it time. People standing in line saw us coming in our Wessenberg outfits (barefoot in the summer), and they let us go ahead, knowing we had a time limit. I enjoyed those quick trips to the city. Even though handling the money was a big responsibility, it was worth it to escape confinement and breathe fresh air for a little while. It was a welcome change from the work routine, even if I often came back out of breath.

Instead of Aunt's August visit, I got a letter from her telling me that she was forced to cancel her trip. A police barricade prevented her from coming to Constance, since it was a border city. Only people living there had the special papers needed to go in. During Aunt's previous visit in July, she had told me that the Allies had landed in Normandy in June. There was great hope for a quick end to the war and full liberation.

FALL 1944

Aunt arrived unexpectedly in September. She made the special effort because I had turned 14, and she knew that I could be moved to a family or to prison at any time. She came to beg Fräulein Lederle not to send me away. The end of the war seemed near. Aunt hoped that once it was over, she would know where to find me.

How Aunt Eugenie had changed! She was gloomy. On our way to visit the Insel Mainau, an isle with a huge botanical garden, she told me about the deplorable situation in Alsace. People were afraid that the Germans would try to defend the Rhine, the natural border between France and Germany. The two armies will meet in Alsace, Aunt explained. People lived in fear. Mulhouse had been bombed. Adolphe's and Marcel Graf's apartments had been damaged. Both families had to move out. The underground activities had ceased not long before. Since the Allies had landed in June, travel conditions had worsened, and it was entirely too dangerous to cross the border.

Aunt explained that her August trip had been interrupted when the police suspected she was trying to escape across the border. They ordered her to go through an inspection. In her girdle were a few pages of the most recent *Watchtower*. Afraid of being caught with the literature, she said she had to go to the bathroom. There she tore the pages into tiny pieces and put some of them in the toilet. The first time she flushed the toilet it did not work. Afraid to flush it again, she ate the rest. A trickle of water at the wash basin helped her to swallow. She was thoroughly searched and had to report to the police in Mulhouse.

Aunt brought more sad news. She was now staying with Grandma and Grandpa at Bergenbach to help out. Grandpa had gone to the village one day to send me a gift parcel, which I never received. Coming back in the heat of the day, he had suffered a stroke and collapsed. He could move around slowly, but his right side was paralyzed. Dad had been moved from Dachau to Mauthausen,* the main concentration camp in Austria. Now Dad never wrote, and

*Mauthausen was a harsh penal camp where inmates were exterminated by means of extremely hard labor. Some prisoners were punished by being forced to carry heavy stone blocks up the "Stairway of Death," a climb of 186 steps from the quarry.

Mother's letters were rare. It seemed that things would get worse, not better, until the war ended.

The war intensified. Aunt couldn't come back; nor could she write. Bombing aggravated the tension. The raids came mostly at night. Bombers flew over Switzerland, heading for southern Germany. Since Constance was on the border, it had the good fortune of being spared.

At night when the siren blew, we had to get up, dress in the dark, and go to the cellar with a gas mask around our necks. The windows were blocked up with heavy sandbags. A single blue light bulb helped us to find the assigned place. Sitting upon benches, sleepy, freezing, and frightened by the buzzing of the aircraft, the little ones moaned and complained. I had to sit at the entrance with a first-aid kit. I had received first-aid training. Our daily chores gave us no time to shed the fatigue of the sleepless nights. Mending always had to be done—clothes, shoes, and stockings couldn't be replaced.

One day while I was mending, I looked out of the window and saw a branch moving. Like a squirrel, a man climbed up, walked along a limb, and jumped over the border fence, injuring himself badly. Quickly the Swiss carried him away to safety. Fräulein Messinger pointed to another tree, a pear tree. German soldiers and dogs had arrived. There was another man up in the tree, and they made him come down. I saw him going by with both hands in the air and a gun in his back. In front of our house, they put handcuffs on him.

Fräulein Messinger came in, standing erect with satisfaction. Proudly she told us that a British spy had been arrested. He had diagrams of Friedrichshafen Hospital. "Those subhumans are even out to destroy our military hospital. But we will win the war. Germany will be victorious. Soon we will have powerful rockets, the V-2, and we will destroy London!"

The war didn't end. For us children, the news blackout made us outsiders, far away from the dreadful reality. When I went to pay bills, I tried to listen to the conversations of the people in line, hoping to hear about the end of the war. Listening to snatches of conversation, I would go from hope to despair. Some wore sad faces full of insecurity and doubt. Others reflected confidence.

Fräulein Messinger spoke fervently about the *Volkssturm*—the plan for German civilians to be armed and ready to defend their neighborhoods in a last-ditch attempt to save the Reich. "This will revive the strength of Germany," she said. "All men under 16 and over 60 are being trained to use hand grenades; even women will be drafted. The factories have produced the greatest amount of ammunition since the war began. Never will enemies set foot upon German soil! There surely will be a battle in Alsace. The Allies will never cross the Rhine!"

❧ ❧ ❧

The Nazi war machine killed thousands, destroying families, cities, fields, and even trees! Our beautiful 100-year-old forest, the lush green wall between Switzerland and us, was sacrificed to the war. No spy would ever again use the trees to escape across the border. Over and over I heard the sound of the ax and the deafening crash of the falling trees. Then came the sound of the saws. Those beautiful oaks, beeches, and firs fell one after another. I mourned each giant as it lay flat on the ground.

I looked upon those men tramping through our garden as plunderers, rapists, and destroyers. Killing those majestic trees—what a shame! Dozens of innocent trees were slaughtered because of one English spy. The trunks were piled high, forming a huge wall around the property. The rest was for our stoves. The scent of the fir trees made me dream of Bergenbach's forest.

The matrons called me. I was designated to saw the branches and the crooked trunks into small pieces. Another girl would take the other end of the saw. They always switched off—Mathilde, Bertha, and Martha—but seldom Hilde, who was Annemarie's favorite. Yet, no one ever took my place. Just two months after my 14th birthday, I was considered an adult. Instead of attending school, I now had to work hard and fast. The mountain of branches and trunks kept me busy for months. The back-and-forth sawing motion kept us warm in the foggy cold air.

"Virtue" was a basic teaching in Nazi schools. Over the years, it was ingrained—each citizen, including youth, was accountable in many ways. An Aryan had to be a hero, having an iron character, tough like leather and quick like a greyhound. We heard it over and over. We constantly heard about our sacred duties. Every girl should aim to become the mother of a German knight. This was the true value of womanhood. Youth needed to learn to go through thick and thin. To be weak, to be soft, was despised.

I didn't intend to be soft or weak. The saw steadily did its work. Sometimes it got stuck and we needed a wedge. The pile to my left diminished, and the one to my right grew, along with my pride.

CHAPTER 9

I Know I Am an Orphan

The cold air invaded the land. A smoky mist floated over the fields, filling the hollows with swirling vapor. The lake reflected the milky sky. Early that afternoon, Fräulein Messinger and I had come over from Constance to buy apples from a farm located behind Meersburg. We had to pass by the castle, walking alongside the vineyard that now stretched out in empty desolation. It looked so different from how it had looked the day I visited there with Mum more than 16 months before and with Aunt just 9 months later. But my memories had faded. I had had no visits, no news, and no letters. The Bible was out of reach. I had no one to talk to. Even my mental pictures of Alsace had started to fade away. Little by little, the shutters were closing on my early childhood.

Work was my salvation. To be a model, a hard worker, irreproachable—that was my only goal. Once I filled my wagon with apples, I had to pull it uphill without enjoying one bite. I perspired, and steam came out of my nostrils. Once in a while, Fräulein Messinger helped me push the wagon wheel out of a hole.

The tower of the castle appeared, along with a sweeping view of the lake and Switzerland. The evening sun changed the colors like a painter—a touch of orange, another indigo. It was the first full sunset I had seen since being brought to Germany. The blazing sky reminded me of my childhood. How often Dad and I had admired the exciting wonder of a constantly changing sky! I felt homesick.

Panic overcame me—fear that I would never see my parents again. Where are they? Are they still alive? Are they suffering? One day, I received a letter from one of

Mum's prison mates. Why didn't Mum write? I suddenly feared the worst. Surely she was dead. Dad hadn't written either; he too must be dead. Maybe Aunt Eugenie was killed in the battle of Alsace, and perhaps Bergenbach was burned to the ground! Frightful images flashed through my mind. I felt faint. Still, I had to pull the apple wagon toward the empty vineyard.

That night, my first time out of prison after dark, I learned that a person can rejoice and mourn at the same time. My heart danced for joy over the beautiful moonlight. But my heart also ached as I contemplated my future, alone.

The streets were almost empty. Our steps echoed. The wagon wheels squealed. I felt uneasy. I gasped at the sound of boots. Before I realized that I was safe, Fräulein Messinger stepped up next to me without a word. As we approached the house, I realized that the Wessenberg home was the only place on earth where I had a haven.

The whole evening, my painful questions bounced back and forth in a vacuum of silence. I felt abandoned, empty, and deprived. I was in a hurry to retreat to my lair, where I could weep silently. My sighing cry to Jehovah was soon quieted. I dropped into an exhausted slumber.

❧ ❧ ❧

Since my outing with Fräulein Messinger, I had changed. I had come back from Meersburg overwhelmed by sadness, certain that I was an orphan. I felt that I was alone and would have to take care of myself from now on. I refused to act like an outcast when I went to town. Why should I walk with my head hanging down? Why should I be scared? And why should I be offended when people tightened their grip on their purses as I—a Wessenberg girl—walked by?

While doing my errands, I usually passed through a desolate field. It had become my favorite shortcut because I could be alone there and could talk to the birds. But today I decided to investigate a place where a convent used to stand. I discovered some black stones, and on them was some old German writing. I deciphered a name—"Hus"— and the words "...and burned alive in this place."

I felt awestruck. I was standing at the very place where a martyr had died. As I gazed at his name, I recalled Dad's account of Johannes Hus, the 15th-century Czech Protestant Reformer. He had been a Catholic priest, a follower of the Bible translator John Wycliffe. Hus was interested in translating the Bible into the vernacular so that more people could read and understand it. With the pope's approval, Hus was convicted of heresy at the Council of Constance and burned alive at the stake on July 6, 1415—exactly at the spot where I stood.

Thinking about Johannes Hus made me think about Marcel Sutter, my dear, dear friend. Marcel had been beheaded as a conscientious objector on November 5, 1943. That stone memorial became a source of renewed strength to me. Whenever I sat there, all alone amid the wild grass, I could meditate. When depression overtook me and I was sent out to pay a bill, I would run to that place and unload my burdens. The martyr's memorial revived my determination to remain loyal to Jehovah.

DECEMBER 1944

Steam filled the room behind the washhouse. Four "phantoms" clothed in long white robes came in and climbed into a tall, dark container, only to disappear. Slowly the vapors settled, revealing us four girls, our nightgowns covering our nakedness. We sat in zinc tubs for a much-needed bath. It felt divine!

The hot water had to be poured in and scooped out by hand. I didn't mind the hard work. The last time we were able to bathe had been during the hot summer months. We had gone to the lake. I was the only one who knew how to swim. I had been proud of it and wrote about it to Dad in the one letter a year I was allowed to send on his birthday. But I never received an answer—I knew that Dad must have died. Now we sat in warm water, washing our bodies under wet nightgowns that stuck like glue to our skin.

Fräulein Lederle handed me a letter. A rich family living in Petershausen, on the other side of the Rhine, had offered to give away a doll. I was dispatched to get it. The beautiful house was built alongside the edge of the Rhine River. Inside, a maid dressed in black with a little white apron and a white headdress looked at the letter. She asked me to wait, and she went inside, closing the door behind her. After all, I was a Wessenberg girl—I might be a dangerous delinquent!

The maid came back with the doll, a little lady half my size, with beautiful auburn hair. Her eyes were blue like my mother's, but they would hide behind sleepy eyelids. Her pink taffeta dress let her lace slip appear, and her hand-knit lace stockings were graced with black leather boots. My little lady wore a beautiful straw hat adorned with flowers and fruit. With white crocheted gloves, she clutched a little handbag, which had a lace handkerchief tucked inside.

On the way home, a bench invited us to sit down by the water's edge. To make my little lady feel at ease, I told her about my doll Claudine—how she had been an obedient daughter, a good student, and a happy child. "Young lady, don't imagine that someone will play with you at the Wessenberg home. You will just sit under a Christmas tree. You'll sit among other dolls, little ones.

"Thirty-eight children will gaze at you. They don't know how to laugh. You may expect playtime, celebration, and laughter, but you'll be disappointed. Finally, you'll be put into a box, stored away in a chest, and locked in a room. You will be let out of prison again next year for two more weeks."

My little lady needed to do some sightseeing, I decided. We went to the Rhine bridge, where we looked down and watched the running water. We didn't stay long. It was cold and damp. We passed the Insel Hotel. We discovered a placard stating that Johannes Hus had been bound in irons there before he was executed for heresy. I told my little lady all about Hus, just as Dad had told Mum and me, and I imagined that my little lady shed tears over the tragedy.

The few passersby slowed down as they approached, looking at us. My Wessenberg dress showed underneath my short coat. Polite smiles and condescending looks greeted the two of us. Some people even seemed to listen to our conversation. My little lady was happy.

❧ ❧ ❧

The sign above the door said *Polizei* (police). A tall green lampshade above the desk shed light on an elderly man who sat there stamping envelopes. He recognized me right away. He asked if I had come to inquire whether he had heard anything. But I stood there motionless, unable to speak. I finally handed him my folded note. There had been a bill inside, but now it was empty. I had lost the butcher's money! I had been in a hurry—I hardly had enough time to go to three stores to pay the bills. I had three invoices with the money folded inside each one. When I got to the last stop, the butcher's shop, his money was gone.

The police clerk recorded my loss in a register book. He also checked another register and found my name, address, and birth date. The entry had been made six months earlier. I had come to the office to turn in a 100-mark bill that I had found. I remembered that all the men working in the office had looked up, curious about the Wessenberg girl. Apparently, "Wessenberg" and "honesty" didn't go together.

But now, things were different. The elderly man said that I had done the right thing in reporting the loss. "Maybe a good soul has found it and will bring it back," he said.

'I can't go back home,' I thought. Surely I would face an angry matron—and punishment. I envisioned my swollen hands and nights without supper. As it was, I was constantly hungry because every day I was doing a man's work.

Almost worse than the prospect of punishment was the thought that I wouldn't be able to go back to visit the Hus stone and his prison cell. I thought a lot about Hus in prison. He had no Bible, and I no longer had a Bible. He kept firm, and I could remain firm too. When I visited that place, I would come back feeling calm, peaceful, and satisfied. But now my visits to these inspiring places might be over.

No one was around when I got back. I spread out the lace tablecloth and put out the plates. But the cups were still sitting in the warming oven. I couldn't stop sobbing, so I decided to stay inside the room and wait for the first matron to appear. I was in trouble—it was Fräulein Lederle!

"You're crying." Turning her head sharply to the tea table she moaned, "You broke those antiques, our irreplaceable porcelain cups!" I looked down at the floor.

"I lost the butcher's money."

"You'll have to pay it back."

"But I have no money."

"Your first salary will pay for it. You shall not be punished. I believe you are honest. I know that some months ago you found a large bill and you turned it in to the police."

Some days later, Fräulein Messinger asked me to get dressed but, as usual, wouldn't tell me where we were going. We called at a house in our neighborhood. The lady was expecting us and invited us in. She waved a bill and said: "Here is the money. I found it in the street just before I got on the train. The police told me that you lost it. I'm happy to give it back, especially to a Wessenberg child who needs to be taught honesty!"

I didn't reach out for the money. Fräulein Messinger did. For a moment I forgot where I was and who stood next to me. Disgusted, I burst out: "I'm not a Wessenberg child! They keep me here because I'm one of Jehovah's Witnesses, because I read the Bible, and because I live by it. My parents already taught me that being honest pleases God. That's why I didn't keep the 100-mark bill I found. I turned it in to the police—you can ask them!"

Fräulein Messinger blushed. The lady was embarrassed. I was happy—happy that the money had been found but even happier that I had spoken up. I had to let them know that Jehovah's Witnesses have high moral principles. Besides, it wasn't often that I got to see Fräulein Messinger dumbfounded!

❧ ❧ ❧

Switzerland's sense of safety disappeared the day Friedrichshafen was bombed. The heavy, continuous bombing and the air-raid sirens frightened everyone. But Fräulein Messinger reminded us, "Germany has that extraordinary power to lift itself out of the ashes!" Fräulein Lederle and Fräulein Messinger continued to conclude their prayers with the words, "God bless our Führer and our Fatherland!"

Life got even harder—the days darker, the food scarcer, and the waiting lines longer. Not only at night but also in the daytime, bombers flew over our heads, and because of them my outings to town grew rare. The constant running into the shelters made us live with a sense of ever-present danger. Up to three times a night, we had to get up, dress, and go to the cold cellar. The days were full of hard work, and sleep was sparse. Schooling was sparse as well.

JANUARY 1945

I had hardly finished with months of chopping wood before Fräulein Messinger found a new job for me. I would be head of a new team of four girls, all of us having reached age 14. It would be smart to plant more potatoes in case of a long siege. So we had to uproot all the tree stumps and make a field out of the former forest. This meant pulling up the big roots, chopping them off, and then prying out the stump with an iron bar. Once we pulled out the stumps, we had to dig up the smaller roots and toss the earth through a sifter.

Hatchets, axes, iron bars—we needed all our strength just to lift the heavy tools. Sometimes two hands were just not enough. We couldn't work very fast. Our strokes were too weak. We had to try again and again. In the end,

though, we got the work done. We were dripping with sweat, we were hungry, and the thin piece of extra bread was not sufficient to calm our hunger.

Days and weeks passed. Gradually, it began to seem that there was nothing left in my mind. I had neither past nor future. It was all gone. Only the present was real, and it consisted of hard labor and scanty food. I was just a beast of burden. And when the evening came, I fell into bed with one worry: Would there be another air raid, another night of broken sleep, getting Anna up and dressed?

I had to go out once more with Fräulein Messinger. Not far away from our street, we called at a house. As we went up to the door, Fräulein Messinger sternly reminded me not to speak. Again, we were expected. The lady of the house greeted me warmly, telling me that she wanted to meet the honest Wessenberg girl. She explained how she had lost a 100-mark bill some time ago, before she had left Constance. Her return had been delayed because of the bombing. She had gone to the police without any real hope of getting her money back.

The lady was profoundly grateful to know that I had turned in her money, and she had prepared a cake and a drink for us. She wanted to know why I was in such an institution. Her questions slowly opened my heart. My weariness vanished. I told her about my training at home, how my parents had educated my conscience according to the Bible and how I had the hope of living on a paradise earth among honest people. I completely forgot that Fräulein Messinger had told me not to talk!

❧ ❧ ❧

Propaganda made the Germans seem invincible, at least in people's minds. In the dark winter of 1944/45, the German people still had high hopes for a stunning German victory. Tales of the V-2 rocket encouraged their belief in the coming of the ultimate weapon—the atomic bomb. Germany, after all, considered itself to be above everyone and everything in the world. Rumors of a total victory came over the wires. People talked of it while standing in lines, and the teachers even taught about it in school. Even though the Allies had crossed the Rhine River, people believed that each German citizen could become a sort of super-soldier if need be.

As the Allies advanced, people's outlook bounced back and forth between frustration and hope. We children dashed down to the cellar at each air-raid alarm, dragging ourselves back to bed as soon as the raid was over. The teachers' hand-held lamps cast moving shadows of us on the wall while we dressed or undressed in perfect order and in total silence. Even during those days of stress, punishment remained a threat. In order to conserve oxygen in the cellar, we were forbidden to talk. The younger ones were so tired they had a hard time staying on their feet. We all became like robots, responding to the noise of the bombers, but living with one desire, the only desire—sleep.

CHAPTER 10

An Unexpected Change

APRIL 1945

The garden work was grueling. We had to turn the ground over. But the days were sunny, and the air was heavy with the perfume of hyacinths. Daisies blossomed, and birds sang. The wonderful fresh air and bright-blue sky were soothing.

One day, we had barely begun our work when the ugly sound of the air-raid alarm sent us running back toward the house. We flung our spades into a corner and ran down to our underground chamber. After checking Anna's dress and shoes, I got my first-aid equipment. I made sure that each child was in her assigned seat. Sitting there in that dim light, with the acrid smell of potatoes in my nostrils, I felt restless and tense. Suddenly, I had had enough. I tore my first-aid kit off my neck and bolted upstairs. The bright light in the hallway blinded me, but I could make out a form standing in my way. It was Fräulein Messinger. Instead of reprimanding me, she said "come" as she started toward the reception room. Opening the door, she said in a monotone, "Maria, your mother is here."

A woman sat at the table. Fräulein Lederle said: "Don't be afraid, Maria. Your mother has been slightly hurt. It's nothing to worry about. She just fell down and injured her face." The woman whom she called my mother was wearing a man's jacket. Her face was bruised, and her skin had red, yellow, and black blotches. She had short, straggly hair, and she hardly smiled. She sat there speechless.

I stood in the doorway and curtsied. Then I left to get my embroidery and other needlework. While presenting my work on the table, I recited my qualifications to be a maid, just as I had been taught: "I can do all housework, cook, wash, iron, and mend. I know how to keep a house and a garden. My needlework is my Sunday afternoon job."

I stood at attention, gazing at the bony hands reaching out for my embroidery. It lay upside down to show the neat needlework on the reverse side. With a painful smile, she put it back on the table. Nodding her head, she asked Fräulein Lederle in a barely audible voice, "Can Simone leave the house?"

This strange woman couldn't be Mum! Her wounded and swollen face had been treated with a red solution and some black powder. The cuts were kept together with little pink strips. She bore no resemblance to my beautiful Mum. The matrons decided that she had to go to court to get a legal paper for my release. They told me to lead her there.

That afternoon, a warm, sunny April day, we walked down the street side by side. I walked because she walked; I kept silent because she kept silent. The strange woman didn't give me her hand; I didn't take hers. My duty was to lead her to the courthouse—that was all.

The first room in the courthouse was empty; so were several others. Finally we came to the right place. The secretary listened to my mother's request. But she said that only the judge could write a release, and he had fled along with all the others, leaving the courthouse nearly empty. Mother's pleas were to no avail.

I saw Mother's personality come alive, as I had always known her. That firm and determined woman was indeed my mother. She was fighting for my legal release. My mother was alive, and she was here!

I wanted to be strong and control my tears, but one tear came. Then, as the dam that I had erected nearly two years before broke down, a flood followed. Mother held me, but nothing could restrain my tears. Once the reservoir of tears was empty, uncontrollable sobbing followed.

Mum brought me back. In front of the Wessenberg home, she reassured me: "Wait until the army comes. It looks like it will be the French. They will be happy to send you off. Just be patient. In the meantime, I'll go to the refugee camp."

Back in the home, the routine resumed—work, alarm, cellar. In bed that night, I had only one desire—a night of sleep without an alarm. But rest was impossible. Instead of alarms, it was nightmares that disturbed my sleep. 'Mother has abandoned me,' I thought. 'She will never come back to get me. That woman was not my mother; that woman is trying to trick me. My mum is dead. I'll stay in Constance all my life.'

In the following days, I tried to sort out fiction from fact. Life continued. Bombers flew overhead. We moved like sleepwalkers, confusing day and night. We faced long hours, even days, behind heavy sandbags in the cellar. Terror filled everyone's eyes. But not my eyes—they must have been dull and vacant.

❧ ❧ ❧

How could this be? Mother had returned. There, spread out on the table, were my school notebooks. Fräulein Messinger and Fräulein Lederle asked if they could keep my notebooks as a model to inspire other children to draw illustrations. Anna asked for my kitchen notebook for her cooking lessons, and Mum agreed.

All my work became the home's property. A Schlachter version of the Bible and the letters I had received were returned to us. I had never seen that Bible before. Mother had sent it to me before she was arrested.

Fräulein Lederle said to Mum, "Frau Arnold, I give your child back to you with the same mental attitude she had when she came." And Fräulein Messinger added: "She was a big help in supervising the children. We never had a problem with her behavior; she set an example for all." She handed me a crystal candy dish, saying: "This is a keepsake of our good memories of you." I nodded thankfully, not quite sure what it meant. Finally, Mum and I left the house. The French army was only a few miles away.

Just around the corner of the Schwedenschanze was the border to Switzerland at Kreuzlingen. A long line of former prisoners headed toward the Swiss Red Cross center. I stayed close to Mum. I was the only child in the line, and we had no papers. The officer looked at us. Mother's face still bore traces of her wounds.

A Red Cross nurse led us to the women's barracks. There we had to get completely undressed. Our clothes were stuffed into a personal bag to be disinfected. We had to line up.

How humiliating! We stood there like animals in a zoo. Ashamed, I tried to hide behind Mum. In line for the shower, I saw that many of the people were scrawny and emaciated. My thick belly and heavy legs made me feel embarrassed. I was horrified to see how skinny Mum was.

After a refreshing shower with lots of suds, we had to report to the doctor for an examination. He questioned Mum about her bruised face. "I fell," she explained. But the doctor wanted details. Her answer was a revelation.

Mother had been in a group of prisoners the SS were taking to Ravensbrück concentration camp. On the way, the SS fled, abandoning the prisoners after locking them in the cellar of an empty farmhouse. The only woman among them was Mum. There was no water or food. They managed to break out, and Mum decided to look for me. A prisoner gave her his jacket. The Germans fled the advancing Allied forces. Mum got into an open truck. Not for long, though. It came under fire from a fighter plane. The truck came to a sudden and violent stop, throwing everyone overboard. That's when Mum hurt her face.

Switzerland at night! We were in a cozy night train heading west. People were polite and kind. Occasionally, the train stopped at a well-lit station. Swiss people handed us coffee, soup, and chocolate—fine Swiss chocolate. Hundreds of hands snatched the gifts through the windows, making the train look like a millipede.

In Geneva, we had to board a French train. The collecting center was in a casino on the French side of Lake Geneva. It served as the checkpoint to enter France. We had been freed of Germany's chains, but we could not leave the casino. All kinds of different examinations and inquiries filled the days.

After listening to Mum's lungs, the head doctor insisted on more details. I then learned that she had been bedridden, close to death from starvation. Had it not been for the help of others—Josephine Laclef's stolen carrots sewn in her sleeves and Rose Gassmann's tiny bottle of milk hidden in the shoulder pad of her jacket—Mum wouldn't have survived the Gaggenau camp. Now I understood why Mum hadn't written to me herself. Rose and

Josephine worked outside the camp and braved the inspection every day. Prisoners caught smuggling anything into camp could face execution.

Rose Gassmann (photo from identity document)

At last we were issued papers to enter France—but home was still far away. It would be a long trip through Lyons and Langres Belfort. We took a cattle train for the first leg of the trip. When the train stopped, we asked to step outside. We were the only women on the train, and there were no toilets on board. The train steps were slippery, and I fell. I bruised my heels so badly that I had to be carried.

Most of the time, I sat in the corner. I was used to total silence. The former prisoners, some moaning, others ranting excitedly, sounded to me like wild people. I felt uncomfortable. What a relief to change trains in Lyons! The regular passenger train slowly advanced to Langres. We felt like we were in a strange land. The French talked so fast, and we had forgotten how to speak the language.

In Langres, the authorities again stopped us. We finally got the necessary legal papers. At last, we would be heading for Mulhouse. I was lying in a dormitory under army blankets. Both of my feet swelled up and throbbed with unbearable pain. The doctor recommended that Mum go home and that I stay in Langres until the pain eased. But I was determined to go with Mum, crawling if necessary. Mum said: "My girl is my responsibility. She comes with me." In the end, they agreed to help me to the train, realizing that no one could tear me away from Mum.

The poor train connections and the long detours delayed us. As we neared Alsace, Mum tried to prepare me for the worst. But she didn't have to. Home for me was wherever Mother was. My only desire was to find Dad, Aunt Eugenie, and the Koehls. The train finally rolled into Mulhouse, ending a journey that had begun 22 months earlier when I had been taken to Germany.

❧ ❧ ❧

The whistle blew as we entered the station, the wheels creaked, and the train let out one last cloud of steam. We were the last ones to climb upstairs to the walkway over the railroad tracks. I broke out in a sweat from the pain.

I was limping along awkwardly when I spotted a solitary, petite lady. She looked dejected as she slowly walked away. It was Aunt Eugenie! I called to her excitedly. She turned toward us in disbelief. She had come to the station every day for weeks.

She ran to her emaciated sister, whose face was unrecognizable. I stood hanging onto Mum. Aunt threw her arms around Mum as they embraced. By the time we got out of the railroad station, we had the answers to most of our questions. Everyone at Bergenbach was all right. The Koehls were in a new apartment and were fine. Angele and her parents had arrived home. We were the last ones to return—except for Dad.

The house at 46 Rue de la mer rouge still bore the scars of the heavy fighting between the French and Germans. On our door were two broken seals. One was marked "Gestapo." They had claimed the apartment as compensation because they had to feed two people in camp! The other seal was from the *Jugendamt,* the organization that had paid for my "education."

Opening our shutters, we found our apartment pretty much as we had left it. Some small pieces of shrapnel, souvenirs of the battle, lay on the floor. They had pierced the shutters and broken the windows. But the management at Dad's factory had already seen to it that the windows were repaired.

Before doing anything else, we offered a deep, heartfelt prayer of thanks to our heavenly Father. Even though Dad hadn't come home, we concluded that since the Mauthausen camp was in Austria, it would take longer for him to return. The Red Cross had established a help center. A board listed the names of the missing Alsatians. Adolphe Arnold was the first name on a long list. The hope that he would somehow make it home on his own prevailed in our hearts. We were going to get everything ready for that happy day.

I asked to sleep alone in my own bed just as I used to do four years ago, before Dad had been arrested. I convinced Mum that I was an adult and wouldn't feel comfortable sharing a bed with her. The real reason was that I couldn't bear to cuddle up to her and feel her emaciated body next to me.

❧ ❧ ❧

Life quickly fell into a routine. Everyone stood in long lines. We still needed tickets to buy food and clothing. Stores remained empty. People wore noisy shoes with thick wooden soles. The bicycles had solid rubber tires. People wore lifeless expressions on their faces. Their liberation from Nazi barbarism didn't erase the bitter memories of war. The memories fueled feelings of grief and even revenge.

Women who had entertained Germans had their heads shaved and had to stand on carts that were led through cities or villages. People administering their own justice killed some who had collaborated with the enemy. I heard that Mr. Ehrlich, the principal, had been tied, naked, to the front of a French tank before it was sent to the German battle line.

We started up our religious activities again. The persecution had stopped, but we didn't have complete freedom. We could hold our meetings but only in private. Still, we delighted to share again in Bible reading and discussion at the Berger's house, in the Koehls' garden, or in the homes of other families. What a joy it was to see that our little congregation had grown! Our hearts overflowed with thanksgiving. We could hardly wait to renew our evangelizing activity.

Among the daily chores was the visit to the Red Cross center at Rue du Fil. The long list of missing persons grew shorter, but Dad's name, the first on the list, remained. Our spirits sank with each passing day. It had been weeks without any news. Special inquiries in Mauthausen yielded no information. Our hopes diminished. Then the day came when the word "missing" appeared next to Dad's name. It meant "presumed dead with no legal proof." The ground seemed to collapse under our feet.

MAY 1945

Walking silently side by side amid blossoming meadows and trees reminded Mum and me of the wonderful resurrection hope. Weren't the blossoming apple trees a sign of the renewal of life after a hard winter? How appropriate were Mum's words: "We know that God cannot lie; he is a living God. If death were able to keep mankind perpetually in its bonds, then it would be stronger than God, wouldn't it?" Our shared faith in the resurrection brought us closer together.

Marcel Sutter's letters helped to calm my innermost turmoil. He had written a letter the day he received his death sentence and another on the day before his execution. I told myself that Dad would have written the same words of faith and consolation if he had been allowed to before he died. I read Marcel's letters over and over again, but deep in my heart, I refused to believe that my father was dead.

❧ ❧ ❧

Was all of this real? Were we really liberated? We could scarcely believe that we were back home, able to make our own decisions and move around without restrictions. The factory owner allowed us to live in the apartment and said that should Mum get her strength back, he would gladly offer her work. In the meantime, he paid Dad's salary. Mother's strength came back slowly, but she had no stamina. She had been dangerously close to death less than six months before.

We now began to learn all over again how to act like civilians instead of prisoners. It took time. We had food again, though it was limited. We had clean clothes, mostly from the Red Cross. We could bathe in warm water with soap—what a luxury! We basked in the intimacy of our home, free to talk, to go anywhere, to open doors or windows, to sit down and read, even to lie down when tired. To us, that was living like royalty. But still there was a void.

CHAPTER 11

A Shadow Comes

JUNE 1945

The doorbell rang. Mum called to me to open the door. There before me stood a delicate Maria Koehl. She whispered, "I'm not alone." Pointing downstairs, she said, "Simone, there is your father!" Stunned and silent, I stood motionless, while my heart danced for joy. But Dad was a pitiful sight. Extremely thin and breathless, he was exhausted by the climb to the second floor.

I wanted to hug him, to fall on his neck and kiss him, but I stood dumbfounded, as if glued to the floor. Dad was barely able to make the last steps. He came close to me but passed by without seeing me!

Mother had quietly come to the door. Mum and Dad fell into each other's arms in a long embrace, tears streaming down their faces. My heart was beating fast. I was happy for Mum, but I felt like an outsider in this exciting reunion. I cried too, yet not for the same reason.

Dad fell down in a chair, limp. After some minutes he looked at me and said: "Are you Simone? I left you as a child!" At that moment I wanted even more to give him a big squeeze, but I still couldn't bring myself to touch him. He looked so weak, so frail, and I was in shock—it was as if he had come back from the dead.

Was this man really my father? How could his voice have changed so? Only four years had passed, but he had become an old man. He had lost his teeth and was partially deaf. His legs could barely carry him; his hands trembled. His round face had become long; his pink complexion had turned yellow. He looked like a stranger to me.

Gradually the story came out. The Red Cross had searched for Dad in Mauthausen, but he had been transferred to the Ebensee concentration camp in Salzkammergut, Austria. There he lost his hearing.

He wore baggy civilian clothes that were given to him at the American military camp in Bad Ischl. After he had been liberated from the Ebensee camp, he had needed medical treatment for many days before he could travel back home on his own. He had boarded the train in Strasbourg. As it passed by our house, he saw that it hadn't been bombed. But he decided to go first to the Koehls' to find out if we had arrived home safely.

❧ ❧ ❧

We planned a family reunion in Bergenbach at Pentecost 1945. We looked forward excitedly to the family gathering. I started thinking about the future, and I felt like a person finally able to get out of a sickbed after months of illness.

Mum and Dad decided that I would go ahead to Bergenbach with Aunt Eugenie. I was relieved. Whenever I heard Dad's dragging feet or saw his lifeless eyes, I felt hurt and crushed. I hated the Nazis for what they had done to him. I wished to get even in all kinds of ways. I welcomed the prospect of going to Bergenbach, to my paradise.

Sitting in the old train, a bundle of emotions, I watched the ruined houses go by as we passed the villages. All I could think about was Bergenbach, with its meadows, its scents, the flowers, and the woods. I would once again run among the ferns and play with the goats. We would turn the clock back.

It started with a sweet night spent alone with Aunt Eugenie. I cuddled with her once again in her bed. The next morning the grass was still wet everywhere. We crossed through the village and started to climb. Then Aunt told me to get my handkerchief quickly—my nose had started bleeding. We walked slowly toward Bergenbach, looking for shade whenever possible. I felt very weak.

I ended up in bed at Grandma's house. Mum and Dad arrived around noontime. I climbed out of bed as soon as I heard Grandma's loud greetings. Grandma gave me one of her special herb tea mixtures followed by a strong coffee with alcohol. Slowly, I began to feel better.

My cousin Angele was back again. She had become a true city girl. She knew how to talk, to play, and to laugh—all the things I had forgotten how to do. Everyone thought it was because of my poor health. I hadn't grown at all during my time in Constance, and I hadn't yet regained my normal weight.

Angele's family told of their experiences in Vichy, the town in unoccupied southern France where Marshal Petain had set up a collaborationist government in July 1940. Dad said how much he had suffered from hunger, especially in Ebensee, where one food ration went to feed four inmates. The others interrupted, saying vehemently: "We *all* suffered from hunger! Now we're together again. Why recall bad experiences? Let's forget the past and enjoy our reunion!" Our family wanted us to treat our wartime experiences almost as if they had never happened.

Father, 1945, four weeks after his release

❧ ❧ ❧

A family photo would memorialize that special day. Uncle Germain, our photographer, kept staring at the wasted figure of Dad and repeating, "Bad, Germany bad." He wanted to take a picture of the three of us, then one of Dad by himself, and finally one of Angele and me. I wanted to go off for a walk with Angele. Someone warned: "Be careful! Don't stray from the path. You may step on a land mine. Just last week someone got blown up!"

Bergenbach was not a safe place anymore. Besides, Angele showed no interest in me. She mainly spoke French, not Alsatian. She talked about her girlfriends and the wonderful time she had had in Vichy. I was silent about my workmates. I had nothing to share. She had been given gifts and fine dresses; I had come back empty-handed. Her schooling must have been exciting; my real schooling had stopped when I was ten. She was full of ambition; I had none. She had boys on her mind; boys were the last thing on my mind. She had become so different from me.

The following day, Mother decided to take advantage of our stay in Oderen to get in touch with a doctor who was there visiting his family. We had not found a doctor who could care for my feet, which I had injured when I fell from the train. They had healed in the wrong position; my feet turned outward, making me walk like a clown. The doctor checked my feet. He was going to correct them the primitive way. He warned, "It will hurt." He was right; undoing and setting the foot back in the right position was a painful experience. He wrapped it in a bandage and let me rest a while, telling me that I was courageous. But had I known that the second foot would be even worse, I would never have let him touch it. He gave me a strong alcoholic drink to dull my senses. He then jerked my foot one way and twisted it just as fast a second time. I fainted from the excruciating pain.

My time back in Bergenbach proved to be far different from the dream of paradise I had expected. Angele's sunny nature made me keenly aware of the abyss that

Simone, Germain, and Angele at Bergenbach

Left to right, back to front: Mother, Father, Valentine, Camille, Eugenie, Angele, Simone, Grandmother, Grandfather

Angele and Simone

Bergenbach

separated us. Back in Mulhouse, the same proved true regarding Blanche, Madeleine, and Andrée. I tried to avoid them whenever I could. I was glad that Ginette had become one of Jehovah's Witnesses, but her visits too made me feel uncomfortable. She was going to a commercial school, and she talked about her grades, her shorthand writing—all in French. How could I make up five years of lost schooling? I felt like an outcast, only capable of sewing, knitting, and keeping house. It seemed that I was destined to become what the matrons at Wessenberg had trained me to be—a maid.

CHAPTER 12

Vengeance or Forgiveness?

"What's all the clamor about?" I asked. It was happening again. Every day, screaming disturbed the eight families living in our apartment house. A woman's hysterical voice would come from the first floor. The awful shrieking made me shiver all over. "Is she crazy?" I asked Mum. "She complains that they haven't come for her yet. Why does she expect to be arrested?"

The answer came when Mother was summoned to the police station. She returned to the place where, on August 24, 1943, she had been arrested at the order of the Gestapo. Now a French policeman triumphantly proclaimed that the time for retaliation had come for Mum. "Here I have the list of your denouncers," he said. "You just sign, and we will arrest them!" The list included the Catholic parish priest, the Protestant pastor, our neighbor Mr. Eguemann, and his wife, our screaming neighbor. But Mum refused to sign. The policeman couldn't understand why, and I too was upset. Didn't her denouncers deserve punishment? Our family had been torn apart and had suffered terribly. My insides boiled.

With time and patience, Mum helped me to understand why she had applied the Bible counsel that vengeance belongs only to God. We would not seek revenge. I thought I had taken my parents' reasoning to heart, until one day Mum returned from a court hearing in Strasbourg. Listening to her account, I again became incensed.

Frau Lehmann, a woman in her 20's, had been in charge of the women's part of the Schirmeck camp. Now she had been brought to court, facing charges of cruel and merciless acts. One of Mum's fellow prisoners related some of the things that Frau Lehmann had done to Mum. Even though Mum could have added much to the list, she chose not to make any further accusations.

I couldn't understand why Mum didn't tell them how Frau Lehmann had taken Mum's civilian work away the very first day she arrived in camp. Then Frau Lehmann gave her a military jacket to mend. Mother refused to work for the war effort and was put in solitary confinement. She was denied bread and water until she mended the jacket. After three days, she was told that the military jacket was not for a soldier but for a male prisoner. Mum then mended the jacket, but she removed the military pleats and shoulder pads. Thereafter, she received only bread and water for several weeks as punishment.

Why didn't Mum tell the judge what had happened when she had used a Bible she had smuggled into the camp to encourage fellow prisoners? Frau Lehmann had beaten the women who listened to Mum's Bible reading, scarring their faces permanently by slapping them with the diamond ring on her finger. Then Frau Lehmann had Mum sent to solitary confinement again. This time her cell was next to the room where the Gestapo interrogated and tortured prisoners. Their blood would trickle into Mum's tiny cell as she listened to their screams. She remained in that cell for three months.

With so much to tell about Frau Lehmann, Mum said nothing to the judge. When asked what she could add to her fellow prisoner's statement, she simply said, "It is the truth." Mum only asked of the judge one thing: permission to approach Frau Lehmann in the courtroom. Mum stood in front of the woman, gazing silently at her. The long, piercing stare must have unnerved Frau Lehmann terribly.

But for me, it was not enough. After Frau Lehmann was sentenced to prison, Mother said to me: "Maybe her conscience will bother her. She is quite young, and in prison she may find time to comprehend her foolishness and repent." This was not the last time Mum astonished me.

Mr. Eguemann, who had once threatened to kill Dad, was now an old man. One day he brought a basket filled with fresh strawberries and tried to give them to Mum. They were piled so high that some of them rolled off and fell on the floor. He gathered them up nervously. Mother steadied the basket and insisted: "I will not take them from you. You're a poor man. Since you have a garden, I will gladly buy whatever you grow. Let me pay for the strawberries." I could not believe my ears.

From that day forward, we had fresh fruit and vegetables from the Eguemanns' garden on our table. Why, even Dad agreed! Had he forgotten that eight years earlier Mr. Eguemann had tried to kill him with an ax? I was constantly amazed at my parents' ability to overcome resentment. They never paid back evil for evil or sought revenge.

But the greatest lesson was yet to come. Mrs. Eguemann was bedridden with terminal cancer. In those days, treatment was sparse. A terrible stench came from under her apartment door. She had no help, no family, and no friends. It wasn't an easy task to wash her and change the soiled sheets, yet Mum did it twice a day for months on end.

In our prayers, we thanked Jehovah that we three were reunited. Nevertheless, Dad was a shell of a man. The doctor seemed unsure about Dad's chances of survival. He was stricken with a severe ear infection. Pain and dizziness drove him into deep depression, and sometimes he had uncontrollable outbursts of anger. Mum nursed him with exceptional devotion. But he couldn't get his strength back.

Mother, Father, Simone

1945

Mother, Simone, Father

1947

Dad appreciated the material help we received from the factory and the Red Cross. He was also grateful for the gift packages and the clothing that came from Jehovah's Witnesses in the United States. But it was hard for Dad to sit around and eat bread he had not worked for. It became a great humiliation for him and another source of stress.

He had many sleepless nights, a carryover from the last camp, where many starving men had turned mad. Some had even become cannibals, attacking dead bodies and dying people. The medication that helped him to sleep couldn't prevent the agonizing nightmares. By morning he would be exhausted.

Dad told us that Brother Eugen Schwab, wearing the purple triangle that identified him as a Bible Student, had saved Dad's life by getting him out of the penal commando unit in Mauthausen. Assignment to that unit often proved fatal. Prisoners were forced to carry 90-pound granite blocks while running up the infamous 186 stone steps of the quarry. Many died while carrying the stones on their backs. If a man dropped a stone, the guards kicked him down the steps to his death, knocking down and injuring other laborers in the process. As prisoners walked along the top of the cliff, SS guards would sometimes single out an unfortunate straggler and throw him over at a spot called the Parachute.

Brother Schwab managed to get Dad transferred to the Ebensee camp to work in the laundry there. Trudging the whole day through a pool of hot water was better than carrying the heavy granite blocks at Mauthausen. Dad frequently spoke about Brother Schwab, thanking God for the Christian man who had saved him from certain death.

Dad seemed like a stranger, not my father. The heavy medication made him walk like a man on drugs. Our outings with him were short. Whenever we encountered a dog, especially a German shepherd, Dad would run away. When greeting people, he would take his cap off and hold it down at his side as if he were facing an SS guard. We didn't have any visitors.

Dad's requests sounded more like orders. He had never been like that before. Mum tried to help me to understand that he had lived through four years of constant orders, harshness, and cruelty. These were the last things he heard before becoming deaf in Ebensee. He had been trudging around in the laundry pool like a living washing machine. An SS man ordered one of the dogs to attack him because he was slow to obey an order. Dad ran and fell on the steps of the pool, and the SS man crushed his face and ears against the stone steps with his boot. That is how Dad lost his hearing.

I also learned that Dad had refused to disguise ammunition boxes by painting dolls on the sides. "I will not lie, not even with a paintbrush!" he told them. They sent him to Dachau's infamous infirmary for medical experiments. He stayed there for six weeks. They tied a cage full of mosquitoes to his left arm so that the insects could feed on his blood. Yet, he never contracted malaria.

Mother patiently told me: "He needs time to heal; Dad needs help. Be obedient, even if it's hard. He is your father."

I was proud of my parents' unwavering loyalty to their beliefs. But how could I reveal to my dear parents that I felt lonely and that my heart ached? How could I add my worries to their daily struggles? I longed for Marcel. So many things reminded me of him. I had started up piano lessons again, but he wasn't there to listen like before, closing his eyes and swinging his foot. Instead, I saw tears in Dad's eyes. My deaf father often walked away in frustration when I played.

Home didn't feel like home anymore. I had expected to pick up my life where I had left off, but nothing seemed the same.

❧ ❧ ❧

Finally, Father's health took a turn for the better. He looked for work, even though he wasn't up to his former job, which was still vacant. He just couldn't carry on a conversation with others, and his hands trembled when he held a paintbrush.

Dad found some design work he thought he could manage at home. It was to be a test. In the beginning, he could only keep his hand steady for an hour, but day after day he improved. This meant that my room became his work studio. I had to sleep amid pots of color.

I applied to the same design school that Dad had attended before World War I. I presented some drawings I had done, and I was accepted. The city agreed to pay the course tuition. I absolutely loved art school!

Dad's strength continued to come back to him, and he used it to teach the Bible; it was his main interest. The strength of his unshakable faith, which had sustained him in the darkest days, was unmistakable. He often spoke of the food packages sent to him at Dachau, especially those that included some "vitamins"—excerpts of *The Watchtower,* hand-copied by Mum and later by Adolphe Koehl and Aunt Eugenie.

Simone , age 17

On the rare occasions when Dad spoke about the horrors of the camp, he described his experiences and also his feelings. He told us about the day that the camp guards summoned him to headquarters for refusing to sign the renunciation of his faith. Jehovah's Witnesses in prisons and camps were often offered freedom if they would sign a declaration, usually a standard form stating that the individual renounced his faith, pledged allegiance to the Nazi regime, and agreed to bear arms and denounce his former religious associates to the Gestapo.

At the camp headquarters that day, the SS had gathered to make fun of Dad, and then they started ridiculing Jehovah's name. Dad stood firm and determined. Then he spoke out, saying with a resolute voice, "Please, Sirs, Jehovah is the name of Almighty God." The guards just stared at Dad in disbelief. Finally one screamed, "Get out!"

"A wonderful feeling of contentment came over me," Dad told us, "an exceptional sense of satisfaction, having stopped those SS men from poking fun at the holy name. I went out expecting to be hanged that same evening."

All the "purple triangles" in the camp with Dad expected him to be executed. The SS never tolerated a prisoner answering back. The Witnesses were sure that the shock of being reproved by a prisoner would push the *Kommandant* to put on a strong demonstration of the SS's authority. But it didn't happen.

I listened with amazement when Dad told about facing the Nazi Lion. He related how he was called to the camp headquarters each time I had refused to heil Hitler and how he reacted when he was held responsible for my decisions. "I felt such a powerful uplift when I heard the SS blaming me for your conduct," he told me. "This news gave me proof of my family's faithfulness."

Dad told how he felt when he heard about my arrest and then Mother's a few weeks later. "I was totally downhearted and wavering in despair. Standing in line for a shower, I kept asking myself, 'Why?' From behind me I heard a man say to someone, 'What Bible text was given to you at your confirmation?' The man replied: 'Trust in the Lord with all thine heart, and lean not unto thine own understanding. In all thy ways acknowledge him, and he shall direct thy paths.'"

"Those words," Dad explained, "were to me like an angel's voice. It was just what I needed to rise out of the depths of despair."

Whenever Dad shared these accounts, tears filled his soft-brown eyes, and he had to take a deep breath before concluding. Listening to my father's expressions of faith—so strong despite his depleted body—impressed and inspired me tremendously. Dad reminded me: "Never give up! Even when you are at your lowest, Jehovah sees you, and he knows what you are going through. He will impart to you the needed strength to overcome the situation and stay faithful. His hand is not short." I knew that he spoke from his own experience.

CHAPTER 13

Precious Hope

A hearing aid for Father arrived, a gift from Witnesses in the United States. What a difference it made! My father's personality was resurrected. His charm returned; so did the twinkle in his eyes and his sense of humor. Little by little, he mastered his trembling. His nightmares subsided; so did ours, even though they never left us completely. Finally, the three of us stopped standing at crosswalks, waiting and waiting for the order, "March!" We didn't jump up anymore when we heard heavy steps coming up our wooden stairs.

Dad's recovery truly helped me to find my own roots. The art school gave me confidence and helped liberate me from the emotional load that I had dragged along with me for more than two years. My returning self-esteem gave me the needed determination to fight my shyness, to overcome my diffident moods, and to take up my goals—to become a Bible teacher and to continue with my artwork.

It had taken almost three years for our wounds to heal, but we had become a happy family again. We needed that time to mend physically and emotionally and to build a solid haven, a house full of sunshine and happiness. Thanks to Dad, I matured into an adult. Thanks to Mum, I had a heart full of enthusiasm.

When I reflect on the past, I have a mental picture of my family that abides in my innermost feelings. We started like a bubbling mountain brook, overcoming the rocky challenges of daily life, running through blossoming meadows, flowing through icy tunnels. Then the joyous stream plummeted over an unexpected precipice. It split into three cascades, smashed against the rocks below, and reached the bottom in a thunderous roar. The foaming waters swirled in a big whirlpool. Eventually the waters collected together again and the tranquil flow was restored—a peaceful stream that brought joy and happiness.

To the end, my parents brought relief and comfort wherever they went. Even during the worst hours, their radiant faces reflected God-given peace, their eyes sparkled like diamonds. Their encouraging, comforting words and good cheer truly were like cool, crystal-clear, life-giving water.

Each survivor of Nazi terror has a unique story to tell. Having a reason to live, to fight, and to endure—these motivations were sources of strength for many survivors. Our family's motivation came from our total confidence in God's promises and the desire to stay loyal to him.

One day, I asked Mum how she was able to endure the disintegration of her family. Without hesitating, she replied: "I had no way to help Dad or you. God held our lives in his hands. When I entered my prison cell, I asked one thing of God: 'Give me strength to turn the page. I want to live day after day and carry each day's burdens.' This is what happened. I was at peace."

How true are the words that Marcel Sutter inscribed in my poetry book: "Hope is the greatest treasure. If a man has lost everything, he still possesses hope!"

AFTERWORD

In 1952, Simone was accepted to the Watchtower Bible School of Gilead in South Lansing, New York. While in New York, she met Max Liebster, who worked at the world headquarters of Jehovah's Witnesses. Max had survived imprisonment in five Nazi concentration camps, including Auschwitz, where the Nazis tattooed the number 69733 on his arm. In coping with the pains of their past, Simone and Max found in each other a companion who loves life and loves people. They were married in September 1956 and since then have lived in France, where they have been full-time Bible teachers for nearly 50 years. Beginning in 1994, Max and Simone Liebster began traveling around Europe and North America, telling their stories and urging people, young and old, to value life and to learn from the lessons of history.

APPENDIX

#1
Excerpts from official inquiry by the courthouse in Mulhouse, March 25, 1943

VI. Life of the minor:

(Report with dates regarding: Child raised by own parents, by relatives, in a stepfamily, or in an institution; attended kindergarten, school, special education, and up to what grade.) Treatment by parents (unloving, abusive), attitude toward parents, severe illnesses, bad association (if these friends have a criminal history, supply names!), criminal history and sentences, morals, list all jobs since leaving school, including apprenticeship, reason for quitting work, pregnancies, etc.

Marie-Simone was raised by her parents. She is physically and mentally well developed. According to her mother, she has always had good reports from school.

Marie-Simone gives a fine impression. She is a quiet and good girl and is well liked by everyone. Her political and ideological education, though, leaves much to be desired. In spring she had to be expelled from school for refusing to give the German Salute. In September 1942, when she should have gone collecting buckthorn berries with her class during school hours, her mother refused to let her go, explaining that this was not compatible with her religious beliefs and has repeatedly shown that she is unwilling to raise her child by the rules of the National Socialist state.

Marie-Simone's education is in such danger that other accommodations are absolutely necessary. On the basis of the Reich Youth Welfare Law, it is warranted to initiate a process to remove the child Marie-Simone and have her raised in an institution of the German Reich.

Mulhouse, March 25, 1943

Signed: Wurch
Representative for Youth Welfare

NOTE: Reichsjugendwohlfahrtsgezetz, enacted July 5, 1922, Section 73 of which made provision for the detention of delinquent children. For detailed background on one such detention facility, see "Der Kleine, der hat sehr leiden müssen Zeugen Jehovas im Jugend-KZ Morigen," by Martin Guse, in "Am mutigsten waren immer wieder die Zeugen Jehovas' Verfolgung und Widerstand der Zeugen Jehovas im Nationalsozialismus," ed. by Hans Hesse (Bremen: Edition Temmen, 1998), pp. 102–20.

#2
Decision of the Lower District Court

XII 21/43 Mulhouse, June 2, 1943

Marie Simone Arnold

Born on August 17, 1930, in Hüsseren-Wesserling, presently living in Mulhouse-Dornach, Rote-Meerstrasse No. 46, legitimate daughter of Adolf Arnold (born on August 22, 1897) and Emma (née Bortot) in Mulhouse-Dornach, Rote-Meerstrasse No. 46, will be temporarily transferred into foster care according to Paragraph 67 of the Reich's Welfare Law.

Reason:

The twelve-year-old has been raised by her parents in the teachings of the "International Bible Students" and has adopted its ideology accordingly. The father is in protective custody because of illegal activities.

Any activity in the teachings of this sect is unlawful.

Since the youth is misled in being raised by sectarian principles, it will result in conflict with basic civic responsibilities and an increasingly decadent character.

Additionally, she represents a danger to her peers.

The requirements for permanent foster care according

to Paragraph 63/I No. 1 of the Reich Youth Welfare Law (RJWG) are fulfilled.

There is danger if the case is delayed.

Lower District Court
Signed: Dr. Menzel, Associate Judge
Registrar:

Mr. Adolf Arnold
Presently in Dachau Concentration Camp

#3
The overseer of the Wessenberg Institution for Juvenile Education

Constance, October 16, 1944

Re: Corrective training of
Simone Arnold from Mulhouse in Alsace

Report of Contact
for the period March 23, 1944, through October 16, 1944

Maria Simone Arnold, pupil in our institution since July 8, 1943, is developing properly in accord with her age and has adapted herself nicely. Initially she often complained about headaches, having repeated bladder infections and pain in her joints. This is all gone. Simone has adapted herself well to the community life of our institution and causes no problems in her training; she is always helpful to other inmates. Bad influence doesn't dare come near her. She is conscientious in doing her homework, and in school she pays attention and is diligent. She tries hard to do her needlework and her house chores. She knows how to keep busy in her free time, preferably by drawing and painting, and she shows talent in this field. A certain dreaminess on her part gives reason for complaint; it is occasionally necessary to awaken her from this state of mind.

(signed) Ch. Lederle

#4
Excerpts from Lebenskunde—Lehrbuch der Biologie für höhere Schulen*
(Life Sciences—Biology Textbook for High Schools)

NOTE: Among a collection of old books belonging to the Sperry family were found two textbooks that were used in Simone's biology classes. The following excerpts are examples of the way the Nazis attempted to indoctrinate German youth with ideals of racial purity and anti-Semitism, providing justification for Nazi programs, such as the T-4 (so-called euthanasia) program, sterilization, and genocide:

Volume 3

Areas of expansion of the human races (p. 26)

It is particularly the remote areas where the previously mentioned *Primitive Races* found their last places of refuge. (Author's italics.) These rather primitive races are physically, as well as mentally, far behind the highly developed races, henceforth leaving a primeval impression....

The most highly developed races are the master races; greater aptitude enabled them to found superior cultures and civilizations.

The law of natural selection (pp. 168–71)

All humans are subject to the iron law of natural selection...

Due to the development of higher cultures, the effect of natural selection was reduced, at times even neutralized.... Natural selection had, in the past, exterminated men ill with severe inherited weaknesses; however, in modern culture these are retained and not prevented from proliferating....

Concerning natural selection, modern culture has worked against nature. It has chiefly perpetuated the survival and propagation of the weakly and sick to the detriment of the one of outstanding ethnic value. What we observe here is sometimes called *Negative Selection, Anti-Selection*. (Author's italics.) In this regard it is important that we realize how swiftly the "ethnic value" of an entire nation can change when left alone to the same degree of selection and anti-selection. Let's assume one half of the population in a nation is less valuable yet produces four children per couple (given the same number of deaths for each group, 15 of 1,000 per annum), the more valuable half having only two children would therefore be extinct within 300 years.

The law of the purity of blood (pp. 172, 173)

How *separate human races* have adapted to different habitats in nature is much more pronounced than in other life forms (Author's italics.). Man has since spread earth wide. This process of adaptation by human races (especially of the three major races) into different realms clearly exposed their physical as well as their mental disposition

It is therefore obvious that the mixing of distant ethnic groups can only be detrimental. They come from a distinct background and naturally have developed within this unique realm in nature. Mixed offspring of them display a physical disharmony, to say the least. This lack of harmony is even more pronounced in regard to the psychological and mental makeup.

The offspring of Negro and Oriental come to mind though uncommon, it can be observed in South America. Not less disadvantageous is the mixing of the White and the Negro. Yet, even the mixing of the White and Oriental races cannot be considered desirable for either ethnic group.

The spreading out of races, markedly of the master races, beyond their original hemispheres, has over time caused a mixing of races, so that at present hardly any race can be considered pureblooded. A partial racial mixture prevalent in a nation can be diverse and of differing value. A specific mixture can be advantageous when a valuable race is dominant and other similar races make up only a certain element. This applies distinctively to the German people. In it the most capable and valuable race, the Nordic race, doubtlessly dominates. This contributes to its basic inner and exterior character. Comparable races blend with it into an inseparable wholeness.

Jews, a racial mixture of parasitic nature (pp. 175–77)

The disharmony of the Jewish racial mixture is apparent also in the frequency of certain diseases. Specifically, the obvious flat feet, among others. Diabetes is four times as common as in other nationalities. But the most repugnant features of the Jewish people root in their mental and moral disposition....

Major characteristics, therefore, are craftiness, physical and mental uncleanness, cruelty, greed, a distaste for physical labor, particularly the vocation of farmer or soldier....

It is therefore right to view Jews as a parasitic nation or a racial mix of parasitic characteristics that causes its host nation only disadvantage and spells disaster. The calamity brought upon Europe initiated by the emancipation of Jewry, which gave them equal civil and political rights, was nearly disastrous....

The Gypsy nation is also a foreign body and consequently has to be rejected....

Above all, it is our sacred and civil duty to protect our blood from being contaminated with alien blood, especially Jewish blood. No greater shame can be inflicted on the honor of the German nation than the breaking of this law.

c) **The intrusion of alien blood** (pp. 192–93)
Homework: Find out the number of Jews in your school district in 1880, 1933, presently!

Next to the decrease in birthrate and an increase in hereditary disease, looms a third danger to the racial integrity of the German people: the intrusion of alien blood. Shortly before and after the world war, Germany became a preferred country of immigration for Jews. From 1910 through 1925 alone, the daily influx averaged 13 Jews into Germany; official figures for Vienna from the period 1920 through 1929 are 26,400. Under the influence of an interpretation of "freedom," called Liberalism, mixed marriages between pureblooded Germans and Jews were on the increase....

A further development is much more ruinous, since these mixed marriages took place among members of the upper educated classes—Jews gained more and more influence in all sectors of daily life. Foremost professions, such as judges, lawyers, theater artists and journalists, were inhabited in shocking numbers by Jews. Since Jewry preferred large metropolitan areas, it was indeed possible that the majority of people holding positions in Berlin and Vienna were Jews....

V. The racial reinvigoration of German blood

National Socialist Germany, as the first country on earth to recognize the mortal danger facing civilized nations on this globe due to a violation of fundamental laws of life, has therefore as a consequence adjusted its policies toward armed combat of these dangers. In correlation of this, the Führer in his speech to the German Reichstag on January 30, 1937, spoke the following significant words:

"For the first time in human history, it became clear in this country that, above all, the most noble and holy cause for humans is the preservation of the purity of blood as given to us by God. For the first time it is possible in this land for people to use the gift of knowledge and discernment as given to them by the Almighty and turn to issues more substantial than victorious wars and successful economic battles. The real revolution of National Socialism has been the tearing open of the Gateway of Understanding and the consequent realization that mistakes and errors of men are temporary and, accordingly, can be improved upon, except one—the significant error of retaining men's blood, of his kind, and its God-given image and God-given characteristics."

1. The elimination of ill and alien hereditary traits

The hereditarily diseased. After the assumption of power by National Socialism, our first concern was to protect the German nation from further increase of hereditarily ill individuals and to reduce to a minimum any further increases. The passing in 1933 of the Law for the Prevention of Hereditarily Diseased Offspring stems from this desire....

This law is an immense blessing and exposes the alternative as something of an unjust, yes, even a cruel, nature. It removes the calamitous results in the absence of natural selection within modern culture and serves us with the aid of advanced science to keep our race clean in a humane way, a method that otherwise is brought about in nature more brutally.

#5
Excerpts from Tromm 1937 (Hitler Youth rally)

More than 5,000 boys and girls
From the public schools
Of the district Heppenheim
Experienced an hour of celebration
On top of the lofty mountain
(signed)
District School Principal

ADOLF HITLER
We are bound only to you!
In this hour we renew our confession:
The sacrifice of the nation
Is my path!
The destiny of the nation
Is my destiny!
The freedom of the nation
Is my freedom!

COMRADES
We are formed of the same blood,
We carry the native soil,
The northern bravery is our guide!
More ancient than churches and monasteries
Is our Fatherland.
Stronger than any baptism
Is our common blood!
Our Reich, you brothers,

Is from this world,
To make it strong
God has ordered us to do.

WE BELIEVE
In the Almighty God in heaven.
He created us,
Leads and directs us,
He is blessing our fight

WE BELIEVE
In this whole world only
In Adolf Hitler.
National Socialism
Is the great faith
Of our nation.

#6
Letter from Adolphe Arnold
Dachau, August 8, 1943

Dachau 3K, August 8, 1943

My dearest ones!

Even though I do not yet have a precious letter from you, I have received with deep appreciation your gifts of love. I have in my hands the parcel containing milk and little muffins, etc., from Eugenie, which brought me great joy. Dear Emma, as far as I know, you are presently with your parents. Please give them my deepest regards. May they also get to know that which brings true peace and also grasp the meaning of the grand times we are living through—and get a firm hold on the real life. Soon the worst will be part of the past.—My Dearest—I would also like to know what Mother wrote in her comforting letter. Since my shoes for summer are far too small, I can't wear them. But sandals or sturdy slippers, size ten, would bring me much joy.

And now you, my most dearly beloved child: Once again, thank you for your brave words, and my fondest wishes for your birthday. Now I truly know that reminders and guidelines are not necessary for you anymore, since you are yourself old enough and God has helped you and formed in you a pure heart; he will also further guide you. As long as we follow our heart, we won't lose our joy, because we have our own judge—our heart. It is this joy that guarantees that our identification of what is good is the right one. It is also the anchor of our lifeboat, and it will bring us safely through the stormy sea. The Lord above us is not slumbering, yet very soon all our longings and hopes will have been fulfilled in a serene reunion of peace and hope. God will accomplish our reunion; we will receive our reward for our work, and he will wipe our tears from our eyes. Let us endure in prayer and faith, for large is the reward of the Lord for those who love him. With his help we can endure things we once considered insurmountable; yes, we even find joy in it. All this will enable us to stay strong; united in love, let us aim for the same goal.

All three of you receive my kisses, especially you, my courageous child. May the Lord bestow peace upon you and happiness and keep you strong until the end.

Your Adophe

Best wishes to the whole family. Especially, though to the beloved one from the garden.

#7
Letter from Adolphe Arnold
Dachau, November 7, 1943

Dachau 3 K, November 7, 1943

My dearest ones,

On Monday, October 25, I received the package with the 12 vitamin tablets. The others arrived also, as well as your news, the letter and the 50 Reichsmarks. I did not receive anything from Valentine.

My dear one, how can I thank you for all you have done? You truly don't shy away from any expense and effort to give me joy, so now I have become one of your greatest debtors, especially to you, dear Eugenie. May the Lord reward you for everything you do for me. The package came at just the right time and caused great rejoicing. If only my beloved Emma could have some of it in her loneliness, but we can only throw everything upon God, for he alone can strengthen us to pass this difficult test. Yes, let us praise the name of the most holy one, for he is cognizant of the ones who love him and he is watching over them in all their ways.

Therefore, we shall walk the assigned path with our focus set only on one goal, God's honor, because only he can rescue. The peace of heart and the joy that the Lord gives are the best guarantee and aid in this difficult time. It should therefore be our utmost concern that we do not lose them. My beloved, once again, I am delighted that the garden is thriving so wonderfully despite the bad weather. In spirit I am constantly with you, and I hope from my whole heart to join you soon in the work. Father surely is enjoying your labor, because he never loved the lazy ones.

So give my cordial greetings to all the dear ones, and let us think of each other diligently in prayer and let us carry one another's burdens in this time period. Then soon we will have overcome all of it.

And now, my beloved child, receive today again my innermost thanks and my wishes for the future from my heart. I am happy that your time is passing by fast. And I pray the Lord will infuse strength and joy into you and that we will see ourselves soon again the Kingdom of Peace, for which we pray daily. And with this thought, I kiss you all again from my heart.

My warmest greetings to the whole family, but especially to the beloved ones from the garden.

Your Adolphe

#8
Letter from Simone to Adolphe Arnold in Dachau
Constance, August 5, 1944

Dear Father,

The much desired letter finally arrived and brought me much joy. How important is the time we live in and how great are the events! I take this opportunity also to write to you for your birthday. This is already the third birthday since we were separated. This is not quite so dramatic, since even so, we are more united. Every second brings us closer to our reunion. As our Lord has led us so wonderfully until this day, for sure he will continue to lead us and if it is to be his will we may be reunited again this year. Let us keep our confidence in Jehovah and keep on in his work and he will surely sustain us. I still have good courage and will keep it up. My greatest consolation is to know that my parents are in God's hands and to know that we are united in prayer, as well as in striving and struggling. I commend you to God's care, under God's protection and hope that soon there will be peace and a happy reunion. I will close this.

Our greatest gift for our birthday would be Peace and Security.

Your thankful daughter,
SIMONE

#9
Letter from Marcel Sutter *
Torgau prison, November 1943

My dearly beloved parents and sisters,

When you receive this letter, I will no longer be alive. Only a few hours separate me from my death. I ask you to be strong and courageous; do not cry, for I have conquered. I have finished the course and kept the faith. May Jehovah God help me until the end. Only a short period of time separates us from the kingdom of our Lord Jesus Christ. Soon we will see each other again in a better world of peace and righteousness. I rejoice at the thought of that day, since then there will be no more sighing. How marvelous that will be! I am yearning for peace. During these last few hours I have been thinking of you and my heart is a little bitter at the thought of not being able to kiss you good-bye. But we must be patient. The time is near when Jehovah will vindicate his Name and prove to all creation that he is the only true God. I now wish to dedicate my last few hours to him, so I will close this letter and say good-bye until we meet again soon. Praise be to our God Jehovah! With my warm love and greetings,

Your beloved son and brother,
Marcel

* Marcel Sutter, conscientious objector, was executed shortly after writing this letter.

#10
Declaration Offered to Jehovah's Witness Prisoners and Camp Inmates

Concentration camp ....
Department II
DECLARATION
I, the ....
born on ....
in ....
herewith make the following declaration:

1. I have come to know that the International Bible Students Association is proclaiming erroneous teachings and under the cloak of religion follows hostile purposes against the State.

2. I therefore left the organization entirely and made myself absolutely free from the teachings of this sect.

3. I herewith give assurance that I will never again take any part in the activity of the International Bible Students Association. Any persons approaching me with the teaching of the Bible Students, or who in any manner reveal their connections with them, I will denounce immediately. All literature from the Bible Students that should be sent to my address I will at once deliver to the nearest police station.

4. I will in the future esteem the laws of the State, especially in the event of war will I, with weapon in hand, defend the fatherland, and join in every way the community of the people.

5. I have been informed that I will at once be taken again into protective custody if I should act against the declaration given today.

.................., Dated ....Signature

INDEX

(Photos and illustrations indicated in italics; an "n" following the page number indicates a reference to a footnote)